Praise for Zoe E. Fox and ACTIVATE YOUR LIGHT

'Zoe E. Fox is an inspirational soul whose personal journey initiated her true path as a powerful intuitive healer and transformative guide. Her calm, luminous presence carries an unshakable strength of spirit that she channels to quickly restore others to wholeness and ease. She is a leader of our times.'

Sonia Choquette, *New York Times* best-selling author of *Trust Your Vibes* and *Ask Your Guides*

'This book will help you heal deeply and remember who you were born to be. It's a book for our times. The world needs you to activate your light, and this book will help you to remember the powerful divine spark that exists within you and ignite a whole new way of being in the world.'

Estelle Bingham, author of *Manifest Your True Essence*

'Activate Your Light *is an elegant, compassionate, and meticulously crafted guide to inner healing and empowerment. Reading Zoe's book feels like being counseled by both a spiritual warrior and a true best friend. She's a deeply loving yet assertive mentor who won't leave your side until you've recognized what's been holding you back and encouraged you to start shining your brilliant light. The crystal-clear guidance of* Activate Your Light *is passionate and practical, rooted in real-life experience of self-healing. This wise, accessible book embraces everyone who hears the call to activate their precious inner light.'*

Sophie Bashford, best-selling author and intuitive practitioner

'This book is your big sister on the healing path that you've been waiting for. Zoe's loving and real voice makes you feel like she's right there with you, ushering you into embodying your light like never before through all seasons of life. Her story shows us that no amount of trauma can ever take away your light, and you deserve to shine, unconditionally.'

Farah Orths, author of *Money Loves Me*

ACTIVATE YOUR LIGHT

ACTIVATE YOUR LIGHT

Heal Your Past
Reclaim Your Energy
Expand Your Potential

ZOE E. FOX

HAY HOUSE
Carlsbad, California • New York City
London • Sydney • New Delhi

Published in the United States by: Hay House LLC, www.hayhouse.com® • P.O. Box 5100, Carlsbad, CA, 92018-5100

A catalogue record for this book is available from the British Library.

Tradepaper ISBN: 978-1-4019-9856-1
E-book ISBN: 978-1-83782-463-2
Audiobook ISBN: 978-1-83782-461-8

1st Printing

Printed in the United States of America

This product uses responsibly sourced papers, including recycled materials and materials from other controlled sources.

The authorized representative in the EU for product safety and compliance is Penguin Random House Ireland, Morrison Chambers, 32 Nassau Street, Dublin D02 YH68, Ireland. https://eu-contact.penguin.ie

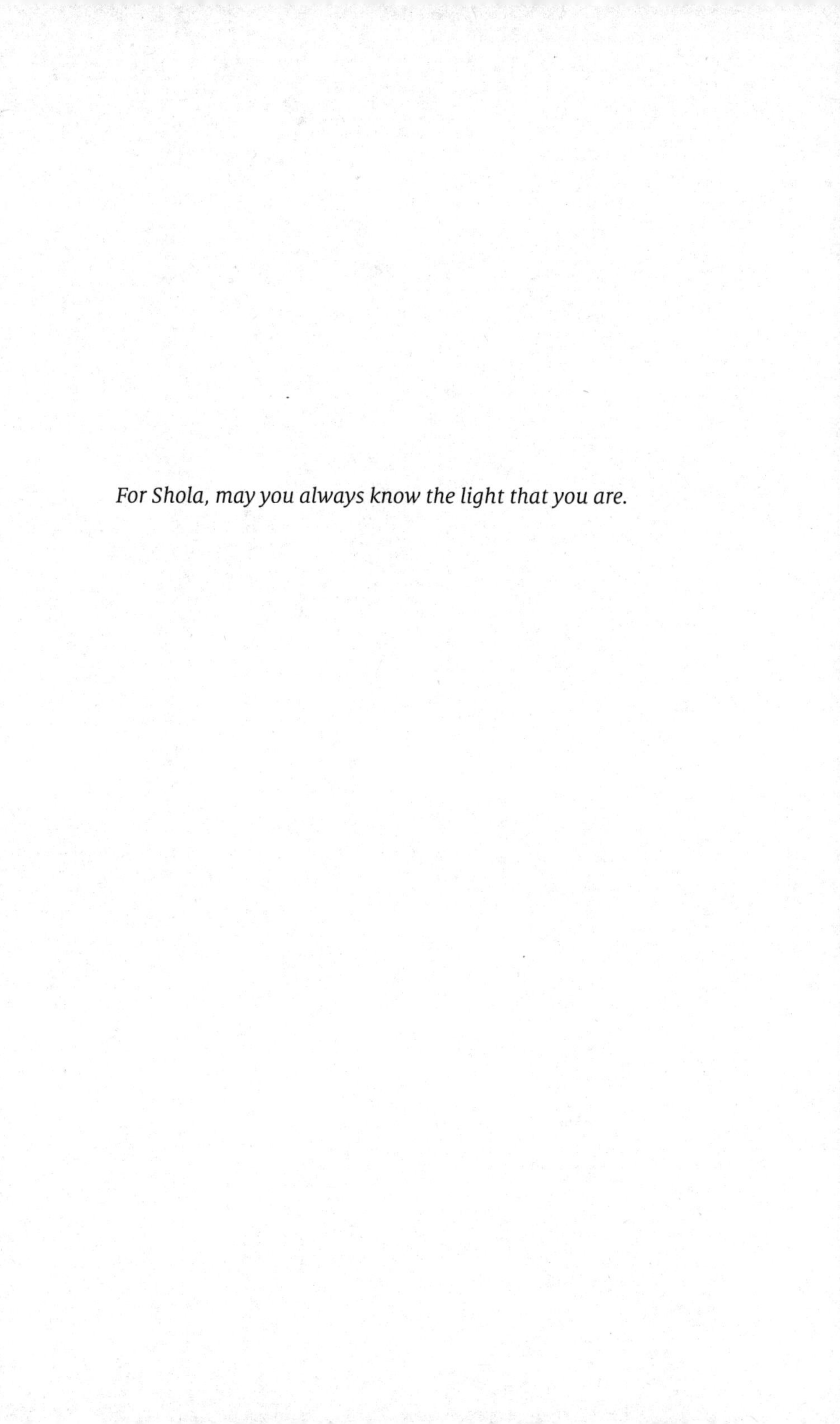

For Shola, may you always know the light that you are.

Contents

PART III Expand

List of Light Activations

Introduction

'On the brink of the death of all that was,
I rise to give birth to all I came here to be.'

What a pleasure it is to meet you here on these pages, at this portal of possibility. This book offers an energetic transmission, which is yours if you wish to receive it. The chances are you've been drawn to it as you are resting upon the cusp of change, and perhaps this sentence will reverberate in your spirit with a sense of recognition that it is indeed time for a new life chapter.

In addition to the changes that we want to see in our own lives, we find ourselves on the edge of a global revolution that seeks to turn the tide on unjust and outdated ways of existence. This will arise in many forms. Some will rebel against the status quo in their might, while others will embody their light.

We all have a role to play.

This book carries the spirit of possibility. The frequency of light woven through these pages will activate and speak directly to the light that *already* exists within you. It will stoke a sense of remembering your true essence.

This journey to your light is born from hard-earned wisdom from a rich life lived, underpinned by the energetics and great spirit that govern our existence.

I write these words from the scars of what were once deep, raw wounds. Wounds that took me on a voyage into my own healing. It was an adventure that elevated me from the darkness of depression, anxiety disorder, PTSD, and purposelessness to the light of great connection, contentment, and waking up with a sense of purpose to a life that keeps on expanding in beautiful, magical ways.

I meet you on this page not from some elevated pulpit of privilege, but from the trenches. I know what it feels like to be stuck, lost in the darkness, and living with physical and emotional pain. I know what it's like to feel unseen, under-represented, and under-resourced. I've known what it is to break down, to grieve, and to feel disconnected from my light. But I've also learned what it's like to heal, rise, and to magnetize a life of beauty beyond anything I could have predicted.

I live with a spinal cord injury and fibromyalgia, so life isn't without its hurdles. But that's why this message is important, because it strips everything away to remind you that here, exactly as you are, you're enough. And from this place, you already have all you need to heal and rise powerfully into your next chapter, even from less-than-ideal foundations.

You don't have to wait for the perfect moment to start reclaiming your light.

Whatever your circumstances, this book is here to help you find light in your shadows and joy in your days. The greatest part of it all is that everything you truly seek is found within.

After over a decade in the darkness, my life was transformed when I finally began to integrate my inner world with the tools of counseling psychology, energy work, intuition, and self-inquiry. Since then, I've used this integrative approach to guide others and have witnessed profound transformations.

I wrote this book because I want you to feel free, free from the weight of what's been holding you back, and open to the beauty of life. This level of healing is what the world needs now more than ever. If more of us followed the process outlined here, we wouldn't just transform our own lives, we'd raise the consciousness and collective experience of the entire planet. Now imagine that.

So how do you do it...?

The Three Stages of Transformation:

1. **Exhale:** Release what no longer serves you; a deep letting go.
2. **Activate:** Awaken your light, connect to your energy, and shift your frequency.
3. **Expand:** Step fully into your power and allow your essence to shine.

Along the way, you'll encounter thoughtful prompts for deepening self-inquiry, as well as Light Activations; powerful energetic exercises designed to help you experience the energetic shifts.

You might like to consume the whole book in one go to catch a vibe before sinking into the activations. To create real and lasting change, however, I recommend working through a chapter a week at your own pace and giving yourself time to sit with the energy of each one, its self-inquiry prompts, and its closing Light Activation.

Get a copy for your bestie or start a book club with your inner circle and activate your light together, connecting on a group call for support along the way. Friends who heal together grow together.

Healing isn't a quick fix, and there's no magic pill. This work does take commitment. You're going to have to want change and be prepared to move toward it. But if you're willing to show up for yourself, be curious, explore, and trust the process, then I can promise you this: you won't recognize yourself a year from now.

So, live in this book. Highlight the pages, fold the corners, make notes, underline what resonates with you, and mark parts to revisit later. If anything helps you, share it with a friend or your online community, and tag me @zoeellenfox. Let me know what's landing for you.

Document your journey by keeping a journal or creating a video diary for yourself. Looking back at your progress and reflecting on your growth can become a powerful source of motivation, and a reminder of how far you've come. You'll have something to look back on and feel deeply proud of.

This is the moment when it all changes, if you want it to.

This is the time to spark the sleeping embers of your soul's light.

So, take a breath.

Let's activate your light.

Big love,

Zoe xx

'May you come to embody a level
of love, belonging, and magical
possibility that emboldens
and illuminates every step
you take toward manifesting
your highest potential.'

PART I

Exhale

Pause · Breathe · Acknowledge · Exhale.

Release everything that is holding you back.

CHAPTER 1

Where Have You Been?

'Your pain is your power. The depths at which you've met yourself have set fertile foundations for you to rise to unprecedented heights. The pain you've endured, the grief you've felt, and the losses you've lived through have all nurtured the soil for your soul's potential to blossom.'

The process of activating your light is a courageous journey through deep layers of awareness, liberating you to come into the fullness of your soul's shining potential. It's a voyage through your past into your present, helping you to bring awareness to the limitations that stand in the way of stepping into the true expansive nature of your soul.

This chapter is about pausing, taking a breath, and allowing yourself to step back and reflect on where you've been, what you've been through, and what you've carried with you until now. The Light Activation at the end of this chapter will walk you through my process for really taking stock of your life thus far. Then you can allow yourself to do something different from what you've always done.

Beginning to Acknowledge Your Journey

We can often be unaware of just how much our past difficulties impact us. As a result of what we've been through but haven't fully processed on an energetic level, we unconsciously form unsupportive thinking habits and automatic patterns of behavior that hold us back from embodying our greatness and block our pathway to activating our light.

Some of life's challenges leave us with physical scars that remind us of what we've overcome, while others can imprint our emotions and leave us energetically scattered. Fragments of our energy become shackled to disempowering moments from the past, and we move through life dragging those stagnant, heavy energies with us.

Many of the people I speak to tell me they feel exhausted as they try to keep up with the demands of our fast-paced world. At some point in their lives, a painful event or series of events reverberated through their inner worlds like a tornado upsetting the landscape, prompting their subconscious minds to create protective patterns to keep them safe. Now, they're doing their best to navigate life while carrying the weight of their own low-vibe energies from the past.

It can be exhausting, like carrying an invisible backpack of bricks everywhere you go.

Do you feel tired? Not just tired in your body, but in your soul.

It's the kind of tiredness that can't be fixed with a nap or a lie-in, a deep energetic exhaustion that comes when we're shackled to the past and not fully embodied in our light.

Is your energy scattered? Have you been carrying the weight of buried emotions, unhealed wounds, and untold stories on top of your daily life's endless demands and pressures? Have you been coping, showing up, painting on your best smile, and pushing through?

The defense mechanisms we set up do work hard to protect us and prevent any further upset to our inner peace. Still, unfortunately, they can run rampant and manifest as restrictive inner voices that keep us small, hemmed into our comfort zone under the illusion of safety.

Over time, as a result of looking away from our pain and trauma, we end up banging our head on the glass ceiling that has formed as a result of our past experiences.

In addition, the heavy and unprocessed energies we're carrying leave us living in a low state of vibration that's unwittingly playing a sorrowful symphony to the universe, in notes that the universe plays back to us. In real terms, that manifests as jobs that don't fulfil us, relationships that don't support us, and situations and circumstances that don't bring us joy.

Do you feel stuck or frustrated that you're
not where you want to be in life?

Do you look out at circumstances that aren't what you really want for yourself?

Perhaps you don't even know what you want because your intuitive voice has been suppressed by what needs to be healed for so long that you've lost touch with your truth and desires.

When disconnected from our intuitive nature in this way, we make decisions based on fear, using protection mechanisms inherited from our past pain. We react to life from the perspective of our fearful and limited self rather than respond from our soul-led intuition.

To begin healing and releasing the past, it helps to bring awareness to your areas of dissatisfaction. This can guide you to aspects of your past that need acknowledgment and healing. There's usually a deeper story attached to the discomfort.

Where in your life do you feel dissatisfied, unfulfilled, or undervalued? Are you a square peg in a round hole at work, or do you give a lot and receive very little in return from an employer who sees you as nothing more than a number?

Is it in relationships that less-than-ideal patterns keep repeating, or is it in the constant people-pleasing that means someone else's needs are always coming before your own?

Your discomfort may be in the quiet moments you avoid by filling your days with endless tasks or distractions – anything to avoid sitting in stillness with yourself. Or is it in the perfectionism, procrastination, and excuses that stop you from moving toward your goals and visions?

When was the last time you stopped to listen to the whispers of your soul?

Maybe deep down, there's a discomfort that comes with stillness that makes it all too easy for you to turn to distractions. When the noise fades, the to-do lists disappear, and you find yourself sitting in the solitude of your own company, what thoughts or feelings start to rise for you?

When we pause and mindfully breathe, we create the space for awareness to descend, like a calming blanket of quiet presence that often feels unattainable when we're wading through the treacle-like residues of our life experiences.

When we pause and connect to our breath, we enter the sweet spot where we can begin to allow our nervous system to stand down, release, trust, and rebuild. So, my friend, I invite you now to pause.

Connect to Your Breath

- Take a long, slow breath in. Let it fill your body. Enjoy the sweetness of arriving in the present.
- Now, slowly release the breath, and with the long, slow exhale, let go of any tension you're carrying in your mind and body.
- Just let yourself land here... fully aware... in this moment... noticing what it is to be present.
- Notice any subtle information that comes forward. Are you becoming aware of any anchors from the past that might be weighing you down?

Holding Space for Your Tender Self

It takes courage to step into the unknown landscape of self-healing and to be willing to confront the pain that we've turned away from or haven't yet had the privilege of healing.

So many souls are craving a soft life in a patriarchal society that doesn't make space for our tenderness and healing. We go through big stuff and are expected to dust ourselves off quickly, get back to work and carry on as if nothing had ever happened. When we find ourselves in survival mode, time for contemplation and healing is a privilege. We push down our pain, suppress our grief, and do our best to keep up with the relentless pace of life.

So, where's the time for our healing?

When we create space in the present and journey inward, we're often met with the energetic residue of our murky past and painful experiences. Many wounded souls abandon their journey here, looking away from their discomfort, not feeling ready or equipped to face their pain, and not realizing the gifts their painful shadows hold when navigated through with loving awareness.

Trust me, you're stronger than you know and have survived your darkest day to date. And the rewards for your courage in confronting your discomfort will be far greater than you can yet imagine.

Once we begin to face what rises in the stillness, we can truly start to reclaim our energy. When we step into our power in this way, we raise our vibration, which is a key component in manifesting our potential.

To truly allow a life of magical possibilities to unfold, I need you to be willing to bring care and compassion to your tender parts so that we can support old, unserving energies in moving through you. Let's rise courageously in the face of discomfort so that we can liberate ourselves to expand beyond the limitations of our stories.

Our challenges can be our greatest teachers if we allow them to be.

Suppressed Emotions Will Demand Attention

For years, I found myself stuck in a cycle of self-sabotaging repetitive behaviors, all rooted in deep emotional pain and a distrust of life that stemmed from witnessing the sudden and tragic death of my boyfriend, G, an event so painful and life-changing I couldn't process the magnitude of the trauma for a long time.

I couldn't face or sit with my raw grief, so I pushed it down and turned away from it. I was in temp work at the time of his death. I couldn't cope with going back to the office, nor could I face going back to our flat, where I'd witnessed him take his last breath. I immediately moved back to my parents' house, and in the first weeks and months following his death, I found it impossible to be left alone.

Every day when my parents left for work, I'd leave with them. Like a slightly less active, grieving Forrest Gump, I'd spend my days walking miles around Birmingham city center, people-watching until my parents finished work for the day. I thought how wild it was that no one knew the emotional turmoil I was in as they all moved through their busy days.

I was too raw to even respond to therapy at the time, so I continued to look away from my pain for over a decade because it was simply too much for me to handle.

Little did I know that in not allowing the energy of my trauma and grief to be witnessed and acknowledged, I created defense mechanisms and energetic blockages that kept me stuck in my pain. Over the years, my grief called out in many ways to be seen so that it could move through me but, ill-equipped, I continued to suppress it.

After G died, I was all too aware of just how suddenly bad things could happen, so that's how I lived, every moment of my waking day, expecting bad things to happen. My traumatized mind made up its own coping strategy by creating rules that would keep me safe. For example, I needed to get on the train at a specific door, sit in a particular seat, and stop driving my car altogether in order to be okay. I became a prisoner in my own mind. Nothing felt safe, not even my daily commute. I was a nervous wreck.

I was diagnosed with generalized anxiety disorder and PTSD that kept me trapped in a limiting and dissatisfying loop. It was like living in my own version of *Groundhog Day*. Every morning, I woke up filled with a palpable sense of dread and a deep fear that permeated my subconscious mind, creating tension in my body and rigidity in my behavior. My suppressed grief and anxiety kept me living really small, firmly within the confines of my 'comfort zone,' which I have to say was anything but comfortable.

Don't Let the Banks Burst

In Dominica, where my momma was born, there's a river for every day of the year. In my family's village, the Colihaut river winds along the edge of the community, bringing life to the landscape, a source to drink from upstream, and a place to bathe and wash clothes in downstream. But during hurricane season, that cleansing body of water is put under great stress. Under the relentless pressure of heavy rainfall, it bursts its banks with a wild force impossible to contain. It has swept away homes, including two of my uncles'. It's a powerful force of nature, and when it's overloaded, it can threaten everything in its path.

Like the river during hurricane season, when life's storms hit, we are put under stress. If we ignore or try to contain the rising waters, they'll inevitably overflow, flooding our inner world and destroying our inner peace, wellbeing, and relationships.

If you consistently suppress your emotions, you'll end up in a whack-a-mole situation, and the suppressed energy will seek some form of expression. Unacknowledged and suppressed emotions can become destructive.

For me, this blocked energy manifested as panic attacks, heart palpitations, chronic inflammation, and a prolonged period of infertility. My body was so overwhelmed by stress that it became a hostile environment for new life to flourish.

How is your past pain manifesting in your life today? Is it in the subtle and unconscious or in the overt and obvious? Is it in the restricted and shallow breathing that prevents you from taking a deeper breath, or in the overstimulated and hypervigilant nervous system that's always on high alert for the next danger?

Is it in the aggression that simmers protectively, or in the ways you feel constantly irritated or emotionally overwhelmed?

Is it in the tension locked in your shoulders or the painful bouts of medically unexplained inflammation in your stomach? Or the health anxiety that keeps you in a state of fear, catastrophizing at the slightest sensation in your body?

Is it in the relationships that feel heavy with unspoken resentment or the inability to fully trust and let love in?

Is it in your hyper-independence and inability to allow support in?

Is it in the fixation with past wrongs that stops you from being present in the now?

Or in the racing mind that replays past wounds, or in the nightmares that disturb your sleep?

Are you afraid to confront the discomfort? Do you find it easier to turn away and live on autopilot, doing things as you've always done?

Facing the Discomfort

When you intuitively know you're here for more, the fear of facing your discomfort can feel like an agonizing state of being stuck. You're tormented by knowing you're meant for something greater, but unsure how to move toward it.

Your soul may whisper of your highest possibilities, but if your ego has its way, you'll resist surrendering to the grander soul plan. And in that resistance, you'll risk missing out on the expansive possibilities awaiting you in this lifetime.

It's not always easy to face up to the part that we play in our own suffering by upholding the behaviors and patterns that keep us small and limited. When we went through our struggles, we did our best with the knowledge we had available to us at the time. Still, things can be different now, as we remind ourselves that we're safe in this moment, and able to confront our tenderness with the conscious awareness and honesty that can set us free from the anchors of the past.

By observing ourselves, our feelings, and our behaviors, we can shine light into the darkest corners of our inner world, the hidden places that have quietly shaped our lives until now.

So, this is where your healing begins. In witnessing yourself, your unmet/unacknowledged needs, and your own story, and in doing so without judgment.

By engaging in mindful moments of self-inquiry, you can observe suppressed emotions, unconscious patterns, and behaviors that may be holding you back.

Self-Inquiry Journal Prompts

Awareness is a practice to be nurtured. Ask yourself these questions regularly, writing your answers down in your journal or on your phone:

~ How am I feeling right now?

~ Is there anything tender or vulnerable at this moment that needs witnessing or holding space for?

~ Was there a trigger for this feeling?

~ Is there some other way I would rather feel right now?

~ What can I do to connect/nurture/align myself more with these preferred feelings?

To nurture the habit of self-inquiry, you can write yourself prompts and place them on doors or mirrors at home. Setting reminders on your phone to nudge you to check in with yourself during the day is also helpful. The key is consistency, not perfection.

You hold the power within to transmute your pain into light and to alchemize your past into the power that will have you living the life your soul knows you're capable of. Let's begin the process together with this first Light Activation.

LIGHT ACTIVATION

Acknowledging Your Journey

When I guide people through this exercise, I love creating a nurturing environment where we can feel held and supported. I love to sit with cocoa tea, a candle, and incense, ensuring we're comfortable in our clothing and at the right temperature.

So, be intentional about creating a sacred space for yourself. Bring your favorite non-alcoholic, comforting drink, best pens, a journal or a big piece of paper (especially if it's been a big life!), and pop your phone on 'Do not disturb.' Better still, leave it in another room. If you have one, safely light a candle to symbolize the light you're bringing to your inner world.

In this space, you'll explore your timeline and the significant moments that have shaped you. These moments might not come in order, and that's okay. Let your intuition guide you.

First, set an intention:

'I set the intention to extract the greatest lessons and blessings from my life so far and to use them as tools for my healing and growth.'

As you map out your life, you might meet parts of yourself that have been hidden in the shadows - unresolved pain, grief, or trauma waiting to be seen. These parts aren't weaknesses to be turned away from, they're the powerful parts of you carrying the weight of survival. They're ready to be acknowledged, honored, and eventually released. Honor the life you've lived so far. Allow *every* version of yourself to be seen, heard, and celebrated.

This process isn't about fixing anything. You aren't broken. It's about shining a compassionate light on the parts of yourself that you've been avoiding.

You're simply bringing awareness to what *is*. Awareness alone is healing.

Before we start, you may want to record yourself reading this activation aloud on your phone - and any others throughout the book - to play back when you're ready, or you can download the audio version of the book from your usual places.

1. **Reconnect**

- Take a few deep breaths to center yourself in your quiet space.
- Visualize a timeline of your life before you - moments rising from the past, waiting to be acknowledged.

2. **Identify the Highs and Lows**

- On your piece of paper or in your journal, begin by marking significant life events, both positive and challenging.
- These could include childhood memories, relationships, losses, achievements, or any experience that left an emotional imprint. Just allow what needs to surface to come to you.

3. **Observe Your Reactions**

- As you write or draw, notice any physical and emotional responses - a smile, a tear, a lump in your throat. These are the energies attached to those moments.
- Allow yourself to feel these sensations if they arise.

4. **Reflect**

- What beliefs or behaviors did these experiences create?
- Gently reflect on how they served you then and how they may no longer serve you.
- Think about any lessons or wisdom that you gleaned from these experiences.
- Are there parts of you still living in the energy of those moments, limiting your growth today?

5. **Inhale, Exhale**

- You might feel some emotions that are light and joyful, and others that are heavier and more uncomfortable. For uplifting feelings, let a color come to mind in connection with each feeling.
- See yourself breathing that color in through your nose, and as the breath fills your body, imagine the colored energy lovingly kissing every cell, nourishing you, activating the light in your cells, and filling you with its high-vibrational energy.
- For any uncomfortable or heavier emotions, assign them a color too. Inquire, notice, or imagine where this heavy energy might be stored in your body. Picture it moving from where it's been stored and leaving your body as you exhale through your mouth.
- Visualize releasing that color as a fine vapor. Let the emotions move like a current without trying to control or change them. Just allow them to be and breathe through them.
- With every exhale, sense a release, creating a sense of lightness within you.

This Light Activation is about more than just self-reflection. As you bring awareness to your journey, you reclaim your power. The past no longer defines you. You are here in the present, ready to rise into the most whole version of yourself.

Welcome in the light of awareness, the light of your truth.

Release, let go, and prepare to rise.

You're no longer surviving.

You're growing, evolving, and stepping into your light.

· ·

CHAPTER 2

That Which Clouds Our Light

'The energetic potency of declaring "Enough is enough!" and beginning the work of reclaiming our light from behind the clouds of our human experience sends ripples into the universe like a rallying call to the higher realms. Our multidimensional glow-up is activated as we reawaken to the path of our higher self.'

We're born naked – sparks of pure light, curiosity, and wonder. But before we take our first breath, the world around us begins to define who we should be. Messages filter into our psyche, impacting our self-perception and how we'll experience, and be received by, the world.

The spark of pure light you came in with will now need to compete for acknowledgment with layers of conditioning. To rediscover the truth of your essence, it helps to become aware of the layers of societal static that cloud your light and how they may manifest in your life.

In this chapter we explore how our outer world impacts our inner world in light-limiting ways. In a reclamation of vibration, thoughts, and feelings, we examine what we consume and how all these things can impact us energetically, and we also begin to bring awareness to how our triggers can be opportunities to know ourselves more deeply.

We accumulate light-limiting layers from myriad sources, including our societal environment and our family lineage. From our family, we can inherit beliefs and behaviors handed down from generation to generation like unwanted heirlooms. They have the potential to condition us with repeating patterns of unworthiness, negativity, struggle, poverty, victimhood, or abuse.

Our ancestors will have formed narratives based on their lived experience and what society prescribed for them throughout their lifetime. In my own ancestry, in the last 200 years, we've had imprints from the trauma of death in childbirth, displacement, world wars, and slavery.

How about you? Is there anything you're aware of in your own lineage that might have impacted your experience today via the impact it had on the generations that came before you? Is your family tree laced with tales of abuse, alcoholism, or addiction? Has the pain of abandonment, infidelity, or fractured relationships echoed through the generations? Have your ancestors endured life-shattering loss and deep grief, the heartbreak of painful separations or difficult divorces, or the burden of financial hardship?

Has racism, discrimination, or displacement shaped the way your family has moved through the world? Are there secrets and lies woven into your history, leaving gaps and unanswered questions that still affect you today?

Multigenerational pain and conditioning continue to reverberate through families until someone finds the courage to examine their inheritance and begin to decode what belongs to them and what has been unconsciously absorbed.

For some of us, our ancestors, recent and distant, faced challenging conditions that threatened their survival. They didn't have the opportunity to decompress or heal. But here we are, born for these times. Times that bring us access to knowledge like never before in history. If we choose to acknowledge our privilege and capitalize on the wealth of wisdom that's available in abundance through affordable books and online resources, we can be the circuit-breakers, the ones willing to confront the discomfort and limitations handed down, by diving head-first into the deep pool of self and ancestral healing.

My spirit knows that if you've been called to this book, you're the courageous one who came here to break the cycle and do the inner work that will move you beyond the human story of the past. You'll transform the energetic signature of your ancestral lineage, redefine *your* authentic path, and set a new blueprint for all possibilities.

With our evolving awareness, we can all begin to deprogram ourselves from the light-limiting societal narratives and inherited restrictions that have held us back until now. But first, let's look at some of the ways we become conditioned in the first place.

Acknowledging Your Conditioning

Did you grow up hearing messages like 'Good things don't happen to people like us,' 'Money doesn't grow on trees,' 'The wealthy are corrupt,' or 'Big houses and nice things aren't for the likes of us'?

Perhaps you were taught that success only came through hard work. Additionally, people of color learned that we should expect to work at least twice as hard to achieve the same recognition as our white counterparts.

Did you grow up in a culture or environment where you were discouraged from talking about your problems or feelings? Did you hear 'Don't cry or I'll give you something to cry about'? Emotions were to be suppressed.

Boys were taught not to show weakness and told not to cry. Girls were expected to be 'good' and not too emotional, bossy, or ambitious.

We absorbed narratives that prescribed a woman's worth as her ability to have children and selflessly serve her family, while a man's success was said to depend on his ability to physically defend and financially provide for his family.

So, the foundations for stifling gender-based expectations were laid.

In some religious households, we learned that we were inherently sinful and any spirituality outside of organized religion was demonic. Earth elements, plant medicines, and aspects of the natural world were stigmatized and labeled as witchcraft. Our connection with Source/God was only considered valid if mediated by an external authority, such as a religious leader, and practiced in a designated place of worship according to a specific set of rules.

We were made to believe we needed to phone a switchboard to connect to the Divine when all along we had a direct line.

Can you see how this can lead to a disempowering sense of disconnection from our own divinity and intuitive nature? Under layers of limitation, we find ourselves shrinking our energy, losing our autonomy, and moving through the world feeling small. We learn to compromise our authenticity in exchange for a sense of acceptance and belonging as we unwittingly conform to societal norms.

In addition to the layers that stem from our homes and communities, we were also influenced by the subtle ways popular culture shaped our beliefs and sense of self in our early years.

Many of us grew up innocently watching Disney's chiseled princes and helpless princesses while playing with blonde-haired, blue-eyed Barbie dolls that embodied impossible beauty standards. From a young age, we were bombarded with advertisements that sold happiness in the form of shiny plastic objects or enticing sugary treats featuring cool kids who all fitted the same narrow mold of beauty crafted in corporate boardrooms that lacked any real diversity at the table.

Revealing the Shadows

My light was clouded by the messages I received from society as a child. Born in 'sin' to parents who were unmarried at the time, I grew up mixed race, working class, in 1980s Birmingham, England, the daughter of a Black Caribbean mother and a White British father. I felt different, and people reminded me I was different, too. I was taunted at school by girls who said my dad was a slave master and my mom his slave. I was called a half-breed and a mongrel and had the 'n-word' with a hard 'er' shouted at me by men in cars as they drove past me in the street.

'You're not like us' seemed to echo everywhere we went. Even when I went to the local hairdresser with my dad and brother, we were turned away and told, 'We don't do that hair here.'

I internalized feelings of shame, rejection, and otherness, and tucked them deep into my subconscious, where they quietly lingered, keeping me limited for years to come.

I looked out at a world where my 'esthetic' wasn't represented or celebrated by Western beauty standards. As a child, I began to resent the brown face that looked back at me in the mirror, and I hated the big, bushy hair that grew out of my head. In a particularly sad moment, I remember whitening my face with talcum powder, desperately trying to see 'beauty' in myself. I was no older than eight at the time.

We'll delve a little deeper into our earliest experiences in the next chapter, but most of us will have at least one memory that springs to mind of an experience that clouded our light.

- Where in life have you had your light limited? Where have you been made to feel less than enough?
- Do you see how our light becomes clouded as impression after impression from the world around us tells us how to look, think, talk, and behave?

When we're disconnected from the source of light within, we seek fulfilment and validation from external sources.

Capitalism rubs its grubby hands together as we consume in an attempt to experience some form of satisfaction, but it's often short-lived.

In our society, fulfilment is sold to us by advertisers, celebrities, and influencers pitching everything from 'perfect' bodies and icy-white teeth to the 'must-have' fast-fashion picks from the identikit human checklist, not forgetting the latest car to symbolize our status. In my own experience, the novelty of the latest car is shorter-lived than the new car smell.

We've been conditioned to keep up with the Joneses in never-ending cycles of consumption, as faceless corporate entities sit hidden away in their boardrooms, pockets fat, empowered by our money, insecurities, and attention.

These corporations are deeply invested in our feelings of inadequacy. Their profits rise when we're disconnected from our innate power and the ever-nourishing source of light within. They shape societal messaging, subtly steering public perception and behavior through mass media that push a consumer-driven agenda. Overconsumption is normalized, and Mother Earth and her most impoverished communities pay the price.

Big tech pillages natural resources in the Congo with impunity, and with their glossy product launches they convince us that it's time to upgrade our devices *again*. Perfectly functioning phones are tossed aside for the latest model because we've been conditioned to believe that we 'need' the highest-quality camera to capture and share, in HD, perfect highlights of carefully curated imperfect lives and material goods on social media.

With HD cameras and high-definition screens comes the desire for picture-perfect skin, so filters are added to photos. But when we look in the mirror, #nofilter, we're dissatisfied with our reflection because it doesn't match the altered images uploaded for the world to see.

We slather hormone-disrupting chemicals onto our hair and skin through popular beauty products that are detrimental to our health. And in increasing numbers, we're lining up at the aesthetician's to pump up our lips and 'fix' our skin with toxic injectables to smooth the frown lines of a face imprinted with the expressions of a life we've been blessed enough to live.

From a wounded place, we pursue perfection. We make tweaks and changes but are often never truly satisfied. It's like an itch that can never be scratched because it's never really about the lines on our forehead, the dents in our thighs, or the narrowness of our lips. It's in the deep, systemic disconnection we've been conditioned into since birth, cut off from our natural beauty and the radiance of our divine light.

When we're struggling mentally and emotionally, it's easy to opt for quick pleasures that distract us from reality, temporarily numb us, make us feel good, or save us some time and energy. Western culture normalizes the vast consumption of vibration-diminishing alcoholic drinks and processed foods, which disrupt our natural balance and deplete our vital energy. These foods are often loaded with chemicals and additives that, over time, take a toll on our body, mind, and spirit. Ingredient lists often contain substances we can barely pronounce or recognize. Companies that prioritize their profit over our health have carefully engineered these products to stimulate our senses, create cravings, and ensure we keep returning for more.

Do you see this web of influence that clouds your light, my friend?

It's a lot. Take a breath.

Once we become aware of how the outside world impacts us, we can start taking steps to return to our power, claim what's ours, and release anything that doesn't belong to us.

What would it feel like to shed these limited ideas of self and reconnect with the truth of who you really are?

It's time to awaken from your slumber. But who is it that lies within, waiting to arouse, and emerge from beneath the programming?

Be willing to indulge the voice within that says you're here for more.

Self-Inquiry Journal Prompts

What does *more* look like? Ask yourself:

~ If I fully trusted my intuition, what would it be guiding me toward?

~ If you don't yet know the answer, to this or any other self-inquiry question, because you've never done it or thought about it, or experienced it, just imagine what it would be like. Through the process of imagining, you begin to cast an energetic spell that reaches out to the universe, energetically aligning with your highest possibilities. So now ask yourself:

~ Where in my life do I feel the stirrings of something greater?

~ Enjoy the romance of getting to know yourself all over again. Watch as sparks of light reignite as the clouds begin to shift and you come to fall in love with the truth of who you are.

As we let go of who they told us we were, we breathe into the light of who we really came here to be.

Taking Control of Your Energy

We can't talk about that which clouds our light without looking at the ways we give away our energy. There are many ways we diminish our light by losing vital energy to different sources, lowering the base level of our vibration. And every bit of energy we give away leaves less for us to manifest our highest timelines.

Without taking control of our energy, we also miss out on the powerful opportunities that arise when we're centered and mindful of where our energy is.

Picture a bucket filled with holes. What's going to happen when you fill it with water? The water will leak out. We're buckets filled with holes. Each hole represents an aspect of where we're leaking energy. The bigger the hole, the greater the loss. It's time to patch up the bucket and restore its capacity.

As you take these steps to observe where you might be leaking your precious energy, you begin to take back control of it. As you evolve in self-mastery in this way, you naturally elevate to a higher state of vibration, the foundation that will support you in manifesting your best life.

So, what holes do you have in your bucket, and where aren't you in control of your energy?

Social media is one of the biggest drains on our energy at this point in history, with growth statistics showing a consistent year-on-year rise in people actively using it. Many of us stack up *hours* daily engaging with these online platforms.

Social media giants capitalize on the fact that our overstimulated nervous systems are uncomfortable in stillness. Many of us are quick to pick up our phone rather than sit and be present with our discomfort.

These companies are literally in the business of competing for our attention. When they have it, they make money. They use a combination of psychological techniques to deliberately keep us hooked on their platforms. Have you ever found yourself opening the app to check your notifications, and the next thing you know, you've been sucked in and doom-scrolling for over 30 minutes?

These platforms can be a hotbed for low-vibrational triggers, from self-comparison to polarizing political opinions. Everyone has an opinion online, and whether you ask to hear it or not, you'll get it. Scrolling is like a game of Russian roulette. You never know when you might come across something that disempowers you.

As we scroll, we can inadvertently hemorrhage our good vibes like water out of a holey bucket. All it takes is one piece of content to trigger us and kill our vibe. The next thing we know, we're in a funk. If we're not mindful, social media can be like a parasite, feeding off our attention, extracting our vital energy, and leaving us depleted and in a state of lowered vibration.

Are you ever conscious of how you're triggered, whether while scrolling social media or in real life?

Is it in the energy of frustration or intolerance when you come across people speaking their truth who don't have the same beliefs as you? Or does witnessing people living their #bestlife online bring up negative feelings in you? A hint of jealousy or a pang of resentment? Does it provoke a sense of inadequacy that dwells within?

Allow triggers that emerge from witnessing someone else living their best life to invite you to live yours. Their light doesn't seek to drown yours out; it serves to illuminate where you've held back from fully stepping into your potential or where you might not be living your life to the fullest yet.

Don't judge yourself, just notice the ways you might unconsciously be giving your energy away. Deploy your courageous, radical self-awareness and allow your triggers to ignite a deeper curiosity within.

Ask yourself, 'What story is attached to these feelings?' Could it be about your own unfulfilled dreams or even about playing small, or feeling stuck in life? Does it bring up past experiences where you were told you weren't enough? Or the scarcity mindset you've internalized from your family lineage?

Where else might you find yourself feeling triggered as you interface with life? Is it when a driver pulls out in front of you, or someone doesn't say 'thank you' when you hold the door open for them? How do you react? Do you feel disrespected or unappreciated? Of course, these moments can be naturally irritating, but do they trigger a disproportionate amount of frustration or even a rage that's not just about that single moment of perceived disrespect?

Does the irritation linger way longer than the encounter itself? Does it play over in your mind throughout the day, perhaps even when days have gone by?

It's here that you may find signs of unresolved emotions or deeper wounds seeking your attention, as when we have wounds around feeling unseen or unacknowledged, we can act defensively, and everyday situations can feel like a deeply personal attack.

Self-Inquiry Journal Prompts

Where do you feel unheard or unseen? Ask yourself:

- ~ In what areas of my life do I feel ignored, dismissed, or misunderstood?
- ~ Are there past experiences where I felt silenced or not listened to, and how might they still be influencing me today?
- ~ What would it feel like to reclaim my voice and be fully seen and heard?

When we surrender to our triggers and environmental factors and allow them to control our responses, we hand over our energy to external circumstances, which can leave us feeling disempowered and stuck in reactive cycles of behavior.

Instead, when situations arise that dim your light, trigger old wounds, or stir up heavy emotions, you can lean into this awareness and observe your experience with compassion. Your evolving awareness will illuminate new opportunities for transformation, even though these moments may sometimes feel emotionally intense or energetically charged.

This conscious presence allows you to process your emotional energy intentionally, choose your desired outcomes, and move through challenges with clarity and purpose.

By de-stressing your nervous system and adopting supportive methods of emotional processing, you remove the light-limiting pressure on your spirit and clear the way to expand into your light.

It's helpful to develop a toolkit of techniques to help you move through the sticky stuff and out the other side of those big emotions, from sadness to anxiety, from frustration to deep rage, or any other emotions that society doesn't hold space for. Here are eight simple and effective emotional energy-shifting techniques to try.

Emotional Energy-Shifting Techniques

1. *Breathe*

Developing a regular breathing practice supports you in nurturing a deeper mind–body connection so that you can center yourself, regulate your nervous system, and begin to unify your mind, body, and spirit. There are many breathing techniques that you can incorporate into your daily practice. Find one that works well for you. Here's one you can try:

The 4:4:4:4 Box Breath

With deep gratitude and respect for India's ancient traditions, and the wisdom-keepers who have preserved and shared these transformative practices, try this breath pattern, which originates from the yogic tradition. Within the tradition, it is known as Sama Vritti Pranayama.

The box breath will help ease your anxiety and bring your nervous system into balance. Follow the steps below and invite calm to your nervous system.

- Have a quiet moment and allow your energy to settle. Relax your shoulders, relax your jaw.
- Inhale for a count of four, allowing your stomach to expand.

- Hold your breath for a count of four.
- Exhale for a count of four, drawing your belly button toward your spine.
- Pause for a count of four before repeating.
- Once the breathing pattern has begun to calm you, place your left hand over your heart and imagine breathing into your heart, acknowledging the emerging sense of calm.
- Now, place your right hand over your left. Notice how each breath draws back more of your power.

This is a practice you can build on. Start small, with just a minute or two each day. In the first week, extend your practice to three minutes, allowing yourself to adjust to the stillness. In the second week, increase it to five minutes.

By the third week, aim to increase your time to 10 minutes. Follow your inner guidance and develop at a pace that is comfortable for you. Gradually increase your time to 15 minutes or longer if your soul calls for it.

....

2. *Cry*

Simple, I know, but you'd be surprised at how many of us apologize for our tears or feel the need to stifle them. Crying is one of the body's most natural ways to release pent-up emotional energy. It's not a weakness, it's a powerful healing force. Those warm, salty, wet tears transmute energy and release what you no longer need.

Let the tears flow freely when you need to cry; don't judge yourself for it. If you're in company, don't apologize for your tears. Notice the shift in your body after you allow the release to flow, and observe how the heaviness lifts, even if just a little.

Afterward, take a deep, nourishing breath and move forward, feeling lighter than before.

3. Rage

Whenever you feel the need to process frustration or rage, just grab a piece of paper, or open up your notes or voice notes app on your phone, and let loose. Write, type, or dictate, and don't hold back. Say everything that's running through your heart and mind. Write with no attachment to keeping any of what you've written. The key here is to let the energy flow through your fingertips.

When the energy has moved through you and you feel a sense of release, take a breath and press 'delete' or rip up your sheet of paper. Symbolically release what no longer serves you. Clear out old energy to make way for the new.

4. Busy Brain Download

When you're dealing with overwhelm at the busyness of your daily life, getting your thoughts out of your head can be the greatest tool for processing the weight in the mind. Writing down or dictating your feelings creates space between you and them. It allows you to observe rather than just react.

Using the page (or your phone app) to decompress and organize your thoughts can be a blessing. Doing this before you sit and breathe or meditate is also helpful if you're prone to thoughts of a million miles a minute, as it helps free up some mental capacity. Pour your heart out onto the paper/app and release your pregnant emotions there. Write/speak as if no one will ever read it. Don't hold back, and don't edit yourself.

Feel the lift once the flow runs dry and the energy has been spent. Don't be attached to your words. They're simply there for the purpose of release.

Once they've served their purpose, feel free to safely and symbolically burn the page, tear it up, or simply close your journal/hit delete and leave it behind.

5. *Write with Intention*

If you ever need to shift stuck energy, just sit down and allow yourself to write freely. Whether it's a letter to someone or an account of a significant day, write without the intention of sending it or giving it to anyone. By writing with the sole intention of expressing yourself, you create a safe space to release and transmute the energy that needs to be acknowledged. This allows you to process and move through emotions without amplifying them, helping you find clarity and healing.

If you feel the urge to send your letter, be mindful that doing so may stir up energy that could prolong or add different dynamics to your healing process. But your soul will instinctively know what's best for you.

6. *Create*

When the banks of your river feel as if they're about to burst, calm your anxiety and bring yourself into the present by channeling your emotions into creativity. Do some art, write a poem, make some music. Do some baking and beat that mixture with extra energy.

Any act of creation turns charged emotional energy into something tangible and beautiful. There's magic in creating when your heart is heavy.

7. Pillow Therapy

Screaming into a pillow or hitting it against the bed is very satisfying when inner rage arises and you want to shift the uncomfortable energy. Your pillow won't judge you, and it won't break.

So, grab that pillow and let it absorb your frustration. Scream into it, launch it across the room, whack it against the bed, use it as a punching bag, whatever helps. (But please, no aiming at people, no matter how tempting! Release the energy in a safe, controlled way.)

Once the pillow's been through it, take a breath and let your body relax.

If the pillow you've used is the one you rest your head on to sleep, hold it in your hands and set the intention to cleanse it of any residual unsupportive energy. Visualize a bright white light emanating from your palms, purifying any residual negative energy and leaving the pillow cleansed and ready to support your resting head peacefully again.

8. Shake It Off

To work through frustration, find a private space, then flick your arms about as if you're having a tantrum.

Visualize or imagine all that excess energy dripping from your fingertips as you wave them around. This is a playful way to release stuck emotions.

If you can visualize the energy flowing out of your fingertips, what does it look like?

What does it feel like?

As you flick away the excess energy, imagine or visualize it being received and cleansed by a bright white healing light that lovingly surrounds you.

When you're done, take a few deep breaths to return to your center.

'Shake It Off' accessibility adjustments

If arm movement isn't an option, try humming at different pitches until you find one that resonates with you. The vibrations can help shift and transmute stagnant energy within your body.

You can also use mental visualization to release energy. Imagine any stuck or heavy energy flowing out with your breath as gray smoke or vapor, dissolving as it's gently cleansed. With each inhale, draw in fresh, cleansing energy, and with each exhale, release what no longer serves you.

• • •

This season of your life is all about the reclamation of your energy so that you can return to your seat of power. When you learn to sit with and observe your triggers and emotions, they can become valuable teachers on the path to self-mastery, signposting deeper areas within your inner world that need to be acknowledged, healed, and released.

Next time you go online, move through your community, interact with your family, or navigate your workplace, observe your internal dialogue and any emotional triggers.

Notice the little voice within that automatically offers an opinion on everything you see. Be aware of each thought that pops up and judgment that creeps in.

Ask yourself: 'What is this emotion inviting me to feel or acknowledge in the shadows of my inner world?'

Gentle awareness, generous compassion, and non-judgment are all that's needed. Be kind to yourself as your awareness expands. It's a crucial part of the process.

When you take control of your energy and begin the transformational process of reprogramming your inner world, you can start to step out from beneath that which clouds your light.

LIGHT ACTIVATION

Reclaiming Your Narrative

Begin to think about the ways in which you may have been influenced by inherited identity and societal limitations. From here, you can begin to cut the energetic cords of the identities and narratives that don't serve you going forward.

- Grab a piece of paper and a pen. Take a moment to center yourself. Take a slow, deep breath.
- Set the intention to let your intuition guide you to see any limiting narratives to be released that don't belong to you, then write down anything that arises.

  Here are some commonly held narratives to inspire your process if you need it:

- We shouldn't talk about our feelings or challenges.
- You don't need to feel happy or fulfilled at work, you just need to work hard and pay the bills.
- You have to look a certain way to be accepted.
- Your worth is based only on your material goods.
- People like us struggle, we don't thrive.
- Don't get ideas above your station.
- Don't shine too brightly, you don't want to make anyone else feel bad.
- Suffering is a part of life. You just have to suck it up.
- Women are meant to stay small, subservient, and quiet.

• Now strike a firm line through each narrative.

• As you're striking through, you can mentally command, 'Delete, delete, delete.' Alternatively, you can visualize the narrative – either the written version or a representation of it – being burned by a violet flame. The Violet Flame is a sacred spiritual fire that supports the cleansing and transmutation of negative energy, clearing the way for higher energies to move through.

• Conclude by therapeutically tearing the paper into shreds.

Now that you've committed yourself to reclaiming your narrative, you can open up to let the most empowered version of yourself begin to be revealed.

. . . .

CHAPTER 3

Inner Child Healing

'I am ready to tend to the most delicate and vulnerable parts of myself, to witness my truth and honor the path that led me here.'

As we exhale and heal the stagnant and stifling layers of our lives, let's turn our gaze to the inner child. The inner child is worthy of special care and attention. They may be small in stature, but their voice can be mighty. They often have a strong desire for safety, acceptance, and unconditional love. When anything threatens their sense of safety, they can retreat, get defensive, or default to familiar behavioral patterns in an attempt to make themselves feel safe. We can be oblivious to the fact that the small, tender, wounded younger self that lives at our core is calling the shots, but many of us will find the inner child in control of how we operate in adulthood.

The inner child is the aspect of us that holds the memories, emotions, and beliefs shaped by our earliest experiences. As we formed our fundamental understanding of the world and how it worked through the narratives we were fed, we may have faced experiences and encounters that ranged from the seemingly insignificant to the deeply traumatic, which created the blueprint for what we would come to expect from life.

While we grow in years, we grow up around our inner child, almost like a Russian doll, often leaving unhealed wounds beneath our protective new layers.

While what we experienced as children might not be present now or true of our current reality, we can still find ourselves responding from the perspective of that wounded inner child.

This chapter and the following Light Activation offer an invitation to reconnect with that vulnerable part of yourself so that you can gently hold space to bring them healing and comfort.

When we work consciously with our inner child to heal their wounds and allow ourselves to be inspired by their playful spirit, a magical equilibrium emerges. When we're guided by their wonder, curiosity, and creativity, we illuminate a pathway of exciting possibilities.

To release our energy from any residual outdated aspects anchored in the past, it's helpful to consider how our inner child may have been wounded and what those experiences meant for them. Then we can update our inner world with new beliefs that reflect who we're becoming.

I think back to a time at Brownies, which is similar to the US's Girl Scouts. I was probably about 10 when I went on my first-ever residential trip. One of the activities on the action-packed weekend was abseiling. As a group, we formed a queue and proceeded to climb up the big wooden structure. One by one, the girls ahead of me clambered over the top of the abseiling frame and descended out of sight like lemmings off a cliff. Suddenly, I was next in line.

I started to feel overwhelmed by the sheer height of the structure and the task ahead. With clammy hands, legs that had turned to jelly, my heart pounding in my chest, and a line of eager girls behind me, I was feeling the pressure as I tried to work up the nerve. A bit of gentle encouragement wasn't enough. The prospect of climbing over the edge and launching myself over the other side proved too much for me. I bottled it. I didn't have the courage to climb over and abseil down. I felt defeated.

The prevailing sense of failure was so loud I never wanted to experience it again, so I became risk-averse. Rather than experience that feeling of failure again, I decided to stay small and safe and never push the boundaries of my comfort zone ever again – well, at least for many years, until I became conscious of my wounded inner child's existence through studying and doing this deep inner work.

From the outside looking in, my 'abseil fail' was a fairly standard, seemingly insignificant childhood experience. That said, it still managed to create restrictive patterns that would reverberate through my life for decades, influencing how I approached challenges and perceived my own capabilities.

As a mother, when I see resistance, hesitancy, or fear in my daughter, I make sure that I take the time to patiently support her and coach her through it. This way we create programs in her inner world of experiencing success and a sense of achievement when she takes herself safely out of her comfort zone.

The Impact of Inner Child Wounds

I connect with people daily who are healing inner child imprints that manifest in a host of different ways, stemming from a wide range of roots – such as growing up in environments where they had to take on duties far beyond their years. Some were landed with taking responsibility for their younger siblings, as their caregivers were wrapped up in the drama of their own lives. They were praised for being dependable and helpful in their parental-support role, while their own childhood enjoyment was on the back-burner. So they learned that prioritizing themselves was selfish. Now they struggle to put themselves first and feel guilty whenever they prioritize their own happiness or needs.

One woman grew up in a home where she had to walk on eggshells. She learned to be hyper-aware of subtle changes in the energy of the environment, knowing that the situation could switch at any moment. She internalized her feelings so as not to rock the boat. Now, living with a baseline level of anxiety, she finds herself putting up with the same behaviors in adult relationships. Still, because this was normalized in childhood, she overlooks red flags and stays in unhealthy dynamics for far longer than she should.

A woman whose childhood wounds were rooted in being bullied carried the scars of that experience into adulthood. Her bully, consumed by their own inner pain and dissatisfaction, couldn't bear to see someone else shine and targeted her as a result. She learned to dim her light to protect herself, hoping it would offer some reprieve or perhaps even acceptance. As an adult, she often hesitates to celebrate her successes or let her light shine fully, fearing it might provoke discomfort, jealousy, or rejection from others.

For another woman, conflict has always been deeply unsettling. Growing up in a home where loud arguments and unresolved disputes were served up as frequently as meals, she began to associate tension with chaos and fear. Her experience left her with no roadmap for navigating conflict healthily. Now, as an adult, she shies away from confrontation at all costs, shutting down at the first sign of tension, which leaves her disempowered to advocate for herself.

Another grew up in a household with a primary caregiver who lacked the emotional tools to provide her with the nurturing and reassurance she needed to feel safe and loved. She felt that love and worth were conditional and to be earned through achievements or good behavior. She became conditioned to overachieve as a way of gaining some recognition and often found herself seeking validation from others to boost her sense of worth. Now she struggles to feel worthy without external reinforcement. And despite constantly striving and working hard, she never really feels that she's enough.

Can you see how the protection strategies we develop in childhood can prevent us from fully stepping into our light as adults? By bringing awareness to these imprints, we can begin to untangle the roots of the past and make space for the empowered, authentic version of ourselves to emerge and lead.

Also, side note, you may find that you're not dealing with a single wound. You may have a *series* of them, stemming back to different experiences in childhood. The inner child can be layered, and as you confront one layer and move to the next level of expansion, you meet your inner child in other areas, too.

So, this often isn't a one-time process. As you go through it, keep an eye out for how your inner child might call out for attention. Be prepared to reassure them wherever their insecurity arises.

Trust that you are a grown-up now and you are indeed safe.

Witnessing the Wounds

You may notice a resistance to inner child work, especially if you experienced significant childhood trauma. It makes sense that you might experience a fear of revisiting painful aspects of a particularly vulnerable time. But you're in control here. This healing happens at your own pace. If you feel you need more help, please seek out professional support in working through your trauma.

If you do feel called to do the work, remember this isn't about dredging up painful parts of your past so that you may dwell there, it's about shining a light into the shadows to see what may be hidden in the darkness. You don't need to set up camp there, just bring compassionate awareness to what you find, so you can witness, heal, and release it.

If you know you're looking back at a particularly painful past, you might find it supportive to anchor yourself in the present. Before you look back, remind yourself of who you are now, your current age, the subsequent challenges you've overcome, and what you've achieved. Visualize roots anchoring you in Mother Earth and let her divine feminine energy provide you with additional holding, strength, and support.

What might you uncover? You might already be aware of events that triggered inner child wounds, but you might also discover less obvious ways they came into being, and you could be totally unaware of how they manifest in your life.

So that you can bring healing to your inner child, let's witness them now, hold space for their concerns, and provide the warmth and reassurance that they need to feel safe and secure.

Check in with yourself intuitively and see what springs to mind.

- Can you think of a time when you felt insecure as a child?
- Do you think back to memories that stand out in your mind that brought feelings of sadness, anxiety, loneliness, pain, shock, guilt, helplessness or uselessness?
- Gently inquire when you first experienced these feelings and allow your intuition to bring forward relevant memories.

You can also observe the symptoms manifesting in your adult experience by asking yourself how you feel or respond to different circumstances. The following exercise may help you:

Self-Inquiry Journal Prompts

Reflect on these situations and notice the first answers that arise for you.

~ I find setting boundaries to be...

~ Letting go of situations feels...

~ Saying 'no' is...

~ Being ignored makes me feel...

~ When I receive a compliment, I...

~ I feel lonely when...

~ I feel hurt most deeply when...

~ Being left out leaves me feeling...

If you did observe discomfort or sadness when journaling around those prompts, can you look beneath the soil at the roots of your response?

The Five Whys

If you're a curious cat like me and you're called to delve deeper, you can deepen your self-inquiry with a technique I was introduced to in my corporate days working at the bank.

The 'Five Whys' technique was developed by Japanese inventor Sakichi Toyoda in the 1930s. It works on the principle that if we ask 'Why' five times, we can drill down beyond the apparent symptoms of a problem to uncover hidden patterns, reveal the fundamental nature of the problem, and identify cause-and-effect relationships.

After leaving the banking sector some years later and pursuing formal studies in counseling, I used the technique in my exploration of healing and the self. Using it to deepen self-inquiry can give you insight into subconscious aspects of the roots of your wounds.

Try it if you feel called to do so and allow yourself the flexibility to ask 'Why' as many times as you need to bring forward clarity.

Self-Inquiry: The Five Whys Technique

~ Using a pen and paper or your phone notes app, write down any of the journal prompts on the previous page and complete the sentence however feels true.

~ Then ask yourself, 'Why?' five times, each time noting down your reasoning.

~ Be sure to stop and take a breath here. Give yourself time and space to exhale through any revelations.

~ Journal out any thoughts and reflections.

LIGHT ACTIVATION

Comforting Your Inner Child

This Light Activation will facilitate a healing, energetic exchange with your inner child. By offering them attention and comfort, you can begin to take control of how you respond to resistance that stems from their tenderness so that you can begin to live a life guided by your soul's light, rather than the limitations of your wounded inner child.

- Find a quiet space where you won't be disturbed, making yourself comfortable in a way that allows your body to relax.
- Take a few slow, deep, calming breaths, relaxing more deeply with each exhale. Feel any tension melt away as you breathe slowly and deeply. Gently close your eyes when it feels natural to do so.
- Now, imagine roots growing from the soles of your feet or the base of your spine and extending deep into the Earth. These roots can also extend from any other part of your body that feels natural and comfortable. They give you a sense of stability, grounding you in the safe and nurturing energy of Mother Earth's womb.
- Imagine yourself standing in front of a beautiful ornate gate. Notice the details - the material it's made from, its color, and the feeling of your hand on it.
- You push open the gate and step into a lush secret garden enclosed by tall walls covered in creeping ivy. It's filled with beautiful flowers and trees, and you're surrounded by the soothing sounds of birds and Mother Nature's healing energy.
- You feel at peace here, safe in this nurturing space. You notice the beauty of the garden, all the colors, textures, and shades

around you, the perfume of the flowers in the air, and the gentle breeze on your skin. You pause to take a moment to drink it all in. Inhale. Exhale.

- As you make your way through the garden, you see a younger version of yourself sitting on a soft blanket on the grass. They look sad. Perhaps intuitively, you know what's at the heart of their sadness. Feeling a deep duty of care, compassion, and love for them, you walk toward your inner child slowly.

- Notice the details of their expression and how they look and feel. What are they wearing? How is their hair styled?

- When you reach them, ask permission to sit down on the blanket next to them. They will be grateful for your presence.

- Take a moment to connect with your inner child. Look into their eyes. If you feel called to do so, hold their hand or give them a cuddle, gently bringing their head to your chest in a heart-activating hug.

- Let them know that you're here for them now and they're safe with you. Breathe for a moment with them and let your connection deepen with each breath.

- Gently ask your inner child what they truly needed in that moment of pain or sadness but didn't receive at the time. Carefully listen to any feelings, words, or images that arise. Honor whatever your inner child shares with you.

- Give them words of love, comfort, and reassurance from a place of conviction. Let them know: 'I see you,' 'I love you,' 'I understand,' 'You're safe with me' – whatever feels good. Imagine giving your inner child just what they need, whether it's a hug, words of encouragement, affirmation, or simply being seen or perhaps even believed.

- Around your neck, you're wearing a crystal necklace that sits over your heart. Notice how it's growing in vibrancy and color. You take it off and pause a moment to observe the texture and color of the activated crystal. What color is it? Carefully place it over your inner child's head. As you do this, their inner light is reactivated by the crystal.
- As they sit in the glow, you visualize, imagine, or sense the child's sadness lifting. Take a breath and exhale.
- You see the light returning to the child's eyes and the smile returning to their face. Their energy and expression have been uplifted. Imagine your inner child feeling secure, loved, valued, beautiful, empowered, and understood.
- Tell your inner child that you love them and are proud of them. Give thanks to them for paving the way for who you're becoming.
- Let them know that the crystal necklace is theirs to keep.
- Ask them if they've any messages for you before you return to the present. Take a moment to listen, notice, or feel.
- In your own way, bring this connection to a close and thank your inner child for being with you today.
- Thank the garden for providing a nurturing and healing space. Walk back through the gate, knowing you can return to this safe space anytime. Take a breath.
- Slowly bring your awareness back to the present moment. Send your energy back into your body by moving it in a way that feels good, or simply through a deep, anchoring breath.
- When you're ready, open your eyes.

Journal your reflections on the experience, any insights into the inner child's world, and any unresolved wounds that may still unconsciously be driving you today.

CHAPTER 4

Can You See the Light in Yourself?

'The formation of crystals occurs over time and under pressure. When you crack open the tough, weathered, rocky crust, you see a crystal's beauty lies in its unique structure and properties, shaped by past conditions. You are a crystal. Reveal your beauty and power.'

As you begin to emerge from beneath the clouds of societal limitations, past challenges, and trauma, who is it that stands blinking in the sunlight? Who is awakening within? Your true essence is preparing to materialize. It's a rebirth. On your terms. In *your* truth.

As you begin to allow your thoughts to expand into new possibilities for your life, the echoes of old limitations can ring loudly in your mind. Our internal dialogue shapes how our reality manifests. It dictates how we see ourselves and what we believe is possible for our life. The more we heal our human experience and connect to our spiritual and energetic essence, the more miraculous our life seems to become. But, if left to run on autopilot, unchallenged, our inner voice can keep us stuck and limited, reinforcing the glass ceilings of limiting societal voices that have long clouded our light.

This chapter invites you to observe the way you speak to yourself and become aware of the unconscious narratives running on autopilot. The Light Activation closes the chapter with a loving ritual designed to help you face yourself with compassion and begin rewriting these inner stories.

It's time for a spring clean. It's time to delete those old limiting programs that take up valuable storage on your internal hard drive, and download a new operating system so that you can begin to access the upgraded wisdom of your powerful, uninhibited, authentic inner voice.

Now is the perfect time to reclaim that inner dialogue so that you can rise into your greatness. Yesterday's done and tomorrow's yet to unfold, but your decisions today will impact your future. Are you going to continue to perpetuate old narratives, or apply your conscious awareness so that you can write new outcomes for your life story?

Self-Perception

In our energetic universe, our level of awareness creates our experience. What we focus on amplifies. Like magnets, we tend to attract people, situations, and experiences that resonate with the frequency of our energy.

How we see ourselves, our self-esteem, and our inner dialogue can influence our circumstances and interactions. When we're in a space of low self-worth, we naturally connect with people and situations that mirror that energy. We might unintentionally align with people and events that feed into our insecurities and self-doubt or reinforce our limited or destructive thinking.

When we open to this understanding, we can self-inquire and examine if or where our low self-esteem, unsupportive inner dialogue, and lack of boundaries are manifesting negatively in our reality. Low self-esteem and poor inner dialogue can make you more likely to settle for less than you deserve because part of you feels that's all you're worth.

Understand that you *can* shift your energy and update your inner beliefs. You're not obliged to stay in the shadows of your past.

You *can* make the shifts to attract a reality that reflects your true worth and light.

Breathe into that, and say aloud or mentally:

> *'I have the power to shift my energy and update my inner beliefs to align with a reality that reflects my true worth and soul potential.'*

Change Your Inner Dialogue

Your inner world is the lens through which you view and experience the world. Like a pair of glasses, if you update your prescription and change the lens, the entire picture shifts. When looking through a lens clouded by insecurity or negative self-talk, you'll focus on everything that validates that. 'Men are trash' – here are some trash men. 'I never win' or 'I'm never lucky' – okay, here are all the ways you're unlucky. 'Bad things always happen to me' – guess what you notice? More evidence for that because that's what your inner world is prescribing. You validate your own beliefs by looking out at the world, seeking proof of your perspective.

What you seek, you shall find.

What if you decided to change your lens? What if you chose to look for new evidence? New evidence that validated your worthiness, validated your potential, and validated the knowing within that's telling you that you're here for more.

Shifting that inner dialogue isn't just about creating a more pleasant conversation inside your head. It's about adjusting your energetic frequency to support how you interact with the magnetic and responsive universe through the language of your vibration.

You emit a unique frequency based on where you're at. Consider your frequency as your personal energy signature. It identifies you based on many factors, including your beliefs, emotions, and state of mind. It radiates out into the universe, magnetizing people, experiences, and circumstances that it resonates with, like tuning in to a radio station or a TV show on a specific channel. While you're watching the horror movie on channel 5, others are simultaneously tuning in to channel 22 to watch an inspiring documentary. Both timelines play out in the collective; what you experience depends on where you choose to focus.

Are you tired of sitting with the lower vibrations of a horror movie? Have you had enough of being on edge and waiting for the next jumpscare? Are you ready to tune in to something more uplifting that'll raise your vibration and inspire and inform you? Just because the TV schedule serves up low-vibe content doesn't mean you need to tune in to it.

Change the channel – choose your timeline.

To change your frequency, you have to be willing to make adjustments in your life. There's no magic wand, and no one's coming to save you, but by taking small incremental steps, you can begin to see reality shift in your favor. By following the process in this book, you're already expanding your awareness and shifting your frequency.

Take the steps, make the changes, and send out messages to the universe that speak of just how worthy and deserving you are.

Magic begins to happen when we make different choices and consciously create from empowered energy.

'I Deserve More'

I was in my mid-20s and at one of the lowest points in my life. Some seven years after the event, I still hadn't fully processed the trauma of losing my boyfriend. It was like I was tuned in to my own horror movie, on edge and awaiting the next jumpscare. I looked through a lens that catastrophized, magnified my trauma, and obsessed over imagined impending disaster. I was lonely in my grief, and my self-esteem was at rock bottom.

Against my intuition, I entered a new relationship from a very wounded place. That relationship quickly became toxic and emotionally and financially abusive. We lived together, and I felt trapped and couldn't afford to leave. The dynamic triggered deep feelings of being unsafe, and my unresolved trauma got to boiling point, triggering severe PTSD. These were my darkest of days. I felt so invisible, so unseen in my inner turmoil. My sanity was crumbling.

My sense of worth was so fractured that I stayed treading water, near enough drowning, in that toxic soup for far too long. No one knew what I was going through – I was too proud and ashamed to admit the circumstances I'd ended up in. I distanced myself from my friends and kept my family in the dark, so no one could see how much I was struggling behind the scenes.

My predicament was a mirror of how I felt about myself. I tolerated the disrespect because I couldn't yet see my value or worth, so I failed to draw boundaries to protect my peace and sanity.

Ravaged by a dark anxiety that took over my life, I couldn't even leave my house without panic attacks setting in. There wasn't even as much as a glimmer of light at the end of the tunnel.

Life felt pointless. It was as if my own mind were against me. My negative thoughts were dominating and detrimental to my wellbeing. I couldn't escape the darkness that consumed me. I didn't know how. I felt helpless and hopeless. I found myself plotting ways to end my life as I stood on the side of the train track on my busy commute home from my city job. It seemed like the only way possible to escape. Thank God I didn't. Thank God a sense of worthiness began to rumble from the depths of the darkness, a rumble that reverberated through my spirit and said, '*Enough!* You deserve better than this, you're worthy of more than this.'

After several years of powerlessness, I knew I had to get to my feet and stand in my power. I knew that I needed to commit to honoring the rumbles of worthiness, proclaiming that worthiness to the universe and saying, 'This ends here. We're done.' I chose myself.

Was it easy? No. Was I scared? Absolutely, but in the following days and weeks, my world began to shift. In choosing myself, I chose a new timeline, and the universe began to shift to support me, starting with making a spare room available for me at my beautiful friend Keyah's house.

I jumped, and the universe caught me.

This was an empowering turning-point in my story. I said, 'I deserve more.' The universe said, 'Yes, you do.'

Within months, a beautiful man called Kane came into my life. He was someone who'd been in my orbit for a while, but now it was time for the stars to align. A gentleman who reflected what I was really worth, he brought love, warmth, safety, stability, and healing, and helped me stand even more firmly in my light. At the time, some said, 'It's too soon,' but my soul knew it was right. This time, I followed my intuition.

Give the universe a chance to serve you your highest timeline by adjusting your inner dialogue and expectations for yourself. Let the universe bring into focus all that's here for your expansion.

If you're to rewrite your narrative, you'll sometimes be required to make difficult decisions, redraw your boundaries, and have uncomfortable conversations with yourself and others. But as you reclaim your inner dialogue, one limiting belief after the next, you'll step out of limiting yourself and into your creative power.

Self-Inquiry Journal Prompts

Where in your life is your inner dialogue resulting in outcomes that are less than you deserve? Ask yourself:

- What recurring thoughts or beliefs limit my potential?
- How does this inner messaging shape my decisions and self-worth?
- If I could rewrite this dialogue, what would I say to myself instead?
- Where in my life am I being called to take charge?
- Are there areas in my life where I'm waiting for permission instead of stepping into my power under my own steam?

~ What have I avoided doing out of fear or self-doubt?

~ If I fully trusted myself and the outcome, what would my next steps be?

The Power of Your Thoughts

We spend our days thinking. Some thoughts float right through our mind like bubbles; they naturally pop and dissipate, and it's like they were never there in the first place. Other thoughts can become stuck and repeatedly resurface. The more energy we feed thoughts with, the more powerful they grow. A simple thought becomes a story, and the story forms part of our beliefs.

So, how do we end up with a limiting belief from a simple thought?

Have you ever been in a situation where your voice wasn't heard and you felt ignored? Like being in a team meeting and keen to contribute, but finding others speaking over you and dismissing your ideas before they had a chance to be heard.

Or perhaps in a medical setting where a doctor has downplayed your symptoms and made you feel over-dramatic, making you doubt your own experiences and intuition?

Or in a personal relationship where you found yourself walking on eggshells, holding back your thoughts and concerns out of fear of conflict or rejection?

At times, we internalize these instances, giving them a greater meaning beyond the incident itself. Our minds make up stories that tell us that our voice doesn't matter, so we don't even try to be heard.

Somewhere along the way, a simple thought becomes something we accept as a truth.

If your parents separated when you were a child, you may have internalized it as the parent that left home was leaving you, rather than leaving a relationship that had run its course. Over time, this could have sown the belief in your mind that you were the cause of the separation, leading you to carry guilt, blame, and perhaps even a fear of abandonment into your adult relationships.

Maybe you had a job interview for a role that wasn't a great match for your qualifications and experience, and you weren't offered the job, and somehow it ended up feeling deeply personal and knocked your confidence. So now you believe that job interviews lead to failure, so you avoid embracing new opportunities.

Perhaps you submitted a proposal to a potential client or a publisher that was rejected because it just wasn't the right business fit for the decision-maker at the time, but you made it mean that you weren't good enough.

One rejection doesn't automatically mean another is inevitable. Failing at something doesn't make *you* a failure. Not winning once doesn't mean you won't win next time. One partner not treating you with the respect you deserve doesn't mean you aren't worthy of love and respect.

Shake off these false narratives.

Switch Your Narrative

Let me remind you that you are not your thoughts. You are worthy. You matter. Your voice matters. Your presence matters. You are more than enough and absolutely deserving. You're resourceful, creative, and so very capable, beautiful soul.

It's time to start believing it.

Let your significance and importance sink into your bones and expand your energy.

Repeat after me:

- 'I am worthy.'
- 'I am enough.'
- 'My voice matters.'
- 'My presence matters.'
- 'I belong here.'
- 'I am capable and deserving of greatness.'

That deep inner knowing that you're here for something more stems from your soul's innate understanding of just how powerful and capable you are.

That rumble in the darkness is a soul remembering.

Are you ready to rewrite your inner dialogue so that you can expand into your soul self, the true source of your inner light? Are you excited and curious about unwrapping your layers of truth and power, like a flower's petals softly opening to the light of the sun?

Think of this moment as ground zero, a turning-point in your consciousness, a place for new possibilities to emerge.

Self-Inquiry Journal Prompts

Rewriting your story. Ask yourself:

- ~ What stories have I internalized about myself that restrict my potential and keep me small?
- ~ What behaviors have these beliefs created?
- ~ Am I willing to release those beliefs, or do they feel intrinsically tied to my identity?
- ~ What could be possible in my life if those stories weren't limiting me?
- ~ What would it feel like to step fully into my light?
- ~ What new behaviors, patterns, and beliefs would I need to embody?

Pull out the weeds, sow new seeds, water them daily, and be amazed by what blooms in the garden of your life.

Celebrate Your Resilience

Do you ever stop to think about what you've overcome, about how you've felt beaten down but got back up, time and time again? Perhaps a little shaken, a little disoriented, maybe even a little dazed, but still you rose. Still, you stood.

When those little voices of doubt and self-criticism creep in, remember your track record. Remember your history of overcoming, how you got yourself up from your knees, time and time again.

Remember the darkness you've been through, the storms you've weathered.

And still you stand. Your light persists.

Take a breath. Feel it as your chest expands with life. With breath, there's life. With life, there's hope. With hope, much is possible.

I invite you to look yourself in the eye and hold space for your tenderness, imperfections, vulnerabilities, and scars.

Celebrate your resilience, your survival, your light.

Find compassion for the person who stands before you in the mirror. Treat yourself kindly and honor yourself with the respect you deserve.

You've survived so much... and still you rise. Powerful soul.

LIGHT ACTIVATION

Mirror Work

This five-step mirror-work activation supports you in breaking free from unhelpful patterns and invoking the new life outcomes you so deserve. Through this process, you'll reconnect with your inner light and empower yourself to step into your creative energy. It gives you the power to nourish your inner world with seeds that stimulate your growth and activate your light.

Set aside some quiet time when you won't be interrupted. Grab your journal and a pen and place yourself in front of a mirror, preferably a full-length one if you have one.

Be gentle with yourself and let this activation guide you back home to yourself.

1. **Reconnect**

- Connect with yourself in the reflection in the mirror and hold your gaze, eye to eye.
- Who do you see? Do you feel self-compassion, or does the inner critic pipe up?
- Breathe deeply and exhale softly, easing into this moment.
- Shift your awareness beyond the noise of the inner critic and tune in to the quiet presence that observes it.
- Ask yourself:

  Who is the one noticing these thoughts? Who is looking back at me through these eyes?

- Notice the separation between you and your thoughts. Your thoughts are like bubbles that float through your mind. You aren't the bubbles, but the observer of them. You aren't the voice that criticizes you. You're the soul awareness that observes as these thoughts arise and pass.

2. **Have Compassion**

- As you look at yourself in the mirror, think about yourself lovingly. What would the unseen and unacknowledged parts of you want to hear in celebration of them?
- Speak to yourself as you'd speak to someone you deeply loved, with compliments and words of praise.
- How does it feel to offer yourself love, kindness, and compassion? Do you feel awkward, or does self-love feel needed?

- Be aware of any inner resistance. Notice any desire to look away. Let negative thoughts fade away like bubbles floating into the distance; alternatively, visualize them dissolving by gently popping them with a crystal wand. Imagine the released energy being harmonized as the bubble bursts.

3. Activate Your Soul

- Expand your energetic interaction with the universe by activating the support of your soul's wisdom. In the mirror, look firmly into your eyes and say:

'Soul, please help me to be reminded of
my true nature, beauty, and light.'

4. Reclaim Your Narrative

- Think about the energies and qualities that you're calling in for your evolution, for example: confidence, prosperity, inner peace, connection to your purpose.

- Write them down, and take a moment with each one, visualizing in your mind's eye what it would be like to embody it. What would it be like if that state of being was with you now?

- While looking at yourself in the mirror, with that sense of amplified energy, speak from the heart, affirming qualities you're ready to embody, for example:

'I am worthy of loving and supportive relationships.'

'I am deserving of an abundance of divine blessings.'

'I am ready to heal, release, and be at peace.'

- Notice any emotions or resistance to the affirmations. Feel those emotions without suppressing them, and let those bubbles float on by.

5. Exhale Outdated Patterns

- Still holding your gaze in the reflection, make the following statements while breathing in deeply to anchor the energy of the affirmation and exhaling to cleanse and release negative energy and outdated beliefs, visualizing gray vapor leaving your mouth:

'I breathe in worthiness and exhale unworthiness.'

'I breathe in fearlessness and exhale doubt.'

'I breathe in trust and exhale control.'

'I breathe in contentment and exhale shame.'

'I breathe in healing and exhale pain.'

- To close the exercise, conclude with 'And so it is' to set the statements into creation.

- Feel the powerful resonance of your words as they shift your timeline and align with your soul's deepest desires. Allow the energy of your declarations to guide you toward the life you're destined to live.

Over the following days, weeks, and months, be aware of your inner dialogue and remember to nourish it with affirmations and to correct unhelpful patterns. You might find it helpful to write your affirmations on sticky notes to place around your living space, like on your mirrors or doors. You could even set them as reminders on your phone to jog your memory of them throughout the day.

CHAPTER 5

Energetic Housekeeping

'With courage, gratitude, and completion, I lovingly release stagnant energetic ties that keep me tethered to past and outdated versions of myself.'

The more we surrender to releasing what no longer serves us in the mental and emotional realms, the clearer we become. With that clarity, we gain deeper insight into what else might be holding us back, including attachments in our physical spaces.

Energetic housekeeping is the process of decluttering and cleansing our home as an energetic extension of ourselves.

A Sanctuary and Foundation

Our home should be our sanctuary. It's where we go to escape from the energy of the outside world, a place where we should feel content and at peace. As we do the healing work, we may find ourselves drawn more than ever to retreat to our nest. In addition to keeping it free from dust and grime, keeping it cleansed of stagnant energy helps us raise our vibration and increase our manifestation potential.

Stagnant energy lingers in the ether, contributing to the energetic 'noise' that clouds our personal energy field. Holding on to objects that no longer serve us or are rooted in past pain or trauma can make us feel energetically sluggish and slow us down on our path to ascension.

We can do the inner work to release and uplift ourselves, but if our environment doesn't support us, it can hold us back, block our blessings, and keep us tethered to the past.

Self-Inquiry Journal Prompt

Consider your home environment and ask yourself:

~ 'How does my space make me feel?'

If the answer is: 'My home makes me feel amazing,' that's beautiful. But if you hesitate or don't feel a full-body sense of contentment with your space, this chapter offers an opportunity to explore that. It also provides supportive rituals and practices to help you release the past and optimize the energy of your space.

First, let's acknowledge that there are circumstances we can change reasonably quickly and others that might be less simple. For example, if you want renovations, decorations, or furnishings that aren't yet in your budget, or you live in an unideal space, give yourself some grace on what's outside your control for now. However, when it comes to energetic housekeeping, we can all take some small steps to raise the vibration of our home.

Release to Renew

As a part of the natural world, we're intrinsically seasonal beings, and a great way to communicate to the universe that we're ready for a new season is through the symbolism and ritual of letting go.

Are you still holding on to dead leaves from past seasons, or do you allow yourself to cyclically release what no longer serves you?

Holding on to physical clutter can weigh down the energy of your space, stifling creativity and disconnecting you from your true self. A stagnant environment can also be symptomatic of deeper discomfort in your inner world that signals unresolved emotions held within.

Conducting a therapeutic audit of your surroundings and allowing yourself to feel what it's appropriate to release at this stage of your evolution is a powerful way to make space to welcome in supportive energies.

Like the phases of the moon, the turning of the tide, and the exhale of a tree as it releases its browned leaves, consider this your season of letting go. Through the uplifting process of energetic housekeeping, you'll amplify your energy by activating the light in your home.

Are You Tethered to the Past?

Do you tend to cling to physical clutter tied to past versions of yourself that, deep down, you know you're ready to release?

Items that clutter your space could include old clothes, expired make-up, broken items that can't be fixed, old receipts or unimportant paperwork from the past, worn-out shoes gathering dust, cables for outdated technology that you no longer own, and birthday cards without sentimental messages from people you're no longer connected to.

For many of us, our phones are in our hands for increasing lengths of time, so let's not overlook the digital clutter that clogs up energetic space in our field. Clearing out unread emails and unsubscribing from newsletters you never read is a great place to start. Other dusty digital corners can include photos that are out of focus, screenshots that no longer hold relevance, or apps that you don't use.

Beyond the Stuff

When you look beyond the stuff and into the emotional residues that these inanimate objects represent, you may unveil attachment issues that are rooted in childhood or traumatic experiences.

Perhaps you find yourself clinging to things you can't quite face, yet can't bring yourself to let go of – objects from a past you can't return to. Or maybe holding on gives you a sense of control in an insecure world.

We may hold on to items symbolic of deeper messages about our sense of worth. For example, the underwear you've demoted to 'period only' pants. Why are they still taking up space if they're too worn out for the rest of the month? Surely you're worthy of quality briefs all cycle long?

Or is it your chipped or cracked tableware? Do you hold on to it because you resist investing in new items? Does this stem from inherited patterns around scarcity or the belief that you must 'make do'? Or does it signal your inclination to hold on longer than you should to things that are damaged beyond repair?

Do you have stacks of paperwork that send you into overwhelm, because they stem from a difficult time in your life and they represent a period that's painful to look back on, let alone organize and shred?

Or clothes from days gone by that don't fit or are perhaps no longer even your style, but remind you of good times before a difficult or traumatic period in your life? Can you trust that good times can come again?

If you're prone to saving those posh candles for a 'special occasion,' have you ever considered that this habit might stem from a mistrust in abundance? The truth is that life itself is a special occasion. You woke up today with breath in your body. That alone is worth celebrating. Light the candles. Use the good stuff.

Know that if your resistance to release stems from a deep-seated fear of lack, holding on too tightly can do the opposite of what you intend, as it signals a scarcity mindset and can keep you stuck in an energy of restriction.

Maybe it's time to let go of those jeans that are several sizes too small, the ones you keep in the back of your wardrobe 'just in case' you fit into them again. Are they really inspiring you to get in shape? Or are they a stick that you use to beat yourself with?

If they genuinely motivate you, keep them, but if they feel like a reminder of what you're not and the sight of them lowers your vibe, set them free.

We'll go through an energetic housekeeping ritual later in this chapter, but for now you can make a start with this journal prompt.

Self-Inquiry Journal Prompt

Check in with your spirit and ask yourself:

~ 'What is it time to release from my home?'

In this decluttering process, I'm not advocating that you should be brutal and part ways with your deeply sentimental and precious items, like your beloved late granny's vase or the lovingly selected and written cards from loved ones, just to be aware of what's hanging around that isn't supporting your energy and growth.

My own journey with energetic housekeeping has been deep and complex. My struggles with letting go are largely rooted in trauma and loss (and perhaps with a hint of influence from my mom, who has a slightly overzealous approach to decluttering: may my 1991 edition Barbie Ski Fun Chocolate Shop rest in eternal peace).

It's fair to say that I've found myself having to part ways with things before I've been truly ready.

After I returned to my parents' house for comfort after G died, our flat sat empty for over a month until after his funeral. I was just too traumatized to return. The flashbacks alone were tormenting enough. The mental challenge of confronting his loss and sorting through his belongings was too much for me in my tenderness.

I eventually summoned the courage to return, bracing myself for the silence that would greet me, but nothing could have prepared me for what happened next.

I put the key in the door and tried to turn it, but it wouldn't turn. I double-checked that I had the right key and tried again, but I still couldn't get in.

On the cusp of where confusion meets panic, I knocked on the neighbor's door. When he saw me, he lowered his gaze. I hadn't seen him since G died. He invited me inside and told me that the housing association had been round, changed the locks, and emptied the flat, dumping what was left of our lives into the communal bins outside.

Apparently, no one had my contact details.

I ran down the stairs and straight outside to the bin shed, desperate to make sense of everything that was unfolding. My chest was tight with nauseating anxiety.

Living a nightmare, I lifted the lid of the industrial-sized bins and peered inside to find just a few bits of our life together sitting in the bottom of a bin like they were worthless, even though they were my everything.

I reached into the grimy container and pulled out G's signature glasses, a couple of his vinyl records, and his favorite designer jumper, which I internally prayed still held his scent.

But that was it. Everything else – our stuff, our memories – gone.

The evidence of our young life together had been obliterated. It was as if it had never existed, had been extinguished before it had even begun.

It felt like I was losing him all over again.

It's not difficult to see how my inner world created stories that letting go equaled loss, vulnerability, and a decreased sense of safety.

Over the years, I've refined my energetic housekeeping process to support my healing and effectively raise my vibration, but the pull to hold on still lingers.

I've learned to give myself grace. Rather than judging or chastising myself, I allow myself the space to honor the deeper roots of why I cling a little tightly to certain things.

Confronting What Needs to be Released

Energetic housekeeping can force us to confront grief on hold, packaged away for a convenient day that never comes and bringing with it a sense of incompletion.

With energy stuck in the ether, waiting to be witnessed and released, we remain anchored to painful episodes. Weighed down by unprocessed and unorganized stuff that creates a low-level irritation to the spirit, it's like a mosquito that buzzes around our ear in the dark.

As I write this chapter, very synchronistically I find myself in the process of energetic housekeeping, where I'm confronted with releasing old identities, and my inclination to hold on tightly is very present.

The last time Kane and I moved house was in January 2020, when we moved into a new two-bedroom flat to accommodate our recently expanded family. Just four weeks after the move, I sustained my spinal cord injury, and shortly after that, we were in lockdown as a result of Covid-19.

At the time, we were firmly in survival mode, adjusting to my disability while raising a one-year-old during the global pandemic. Kane had managed to unpack our essentials, but we didn't have the mental space or inner resources to unpack the rest of the boxes from our life in our one-bedroom flat, so Kane carefully put them away in the attic, promising that we'd unpack them when things got a little easier.

It would be several years before we looked through those boxes again.

Just the other day, Kane ventured into the attic and, a stack at a time, I was reunited with dusty boxes of forgotten items that I'd enthusiastically packed away, all excited about a new life in a new home. Totally unaware of the trauma that waited for us around the corner.

As I began to sort through, grief and loss jumped out at me like a jack-in-the-box. Not only did I find myself grieving the changes to my body, but also the grief of having been thrown abruptly into the world of spinal cord injury when I should have been focused on enjoying my long-awaited motherhood and our beautiful baby girl. Instead, I found myself learning to walk again while she was taking her first steps.

As I worked my way through the boxes, I found myself crying over a vegetable steamer. I'd used it to cook my daughter Shola's first foods before our lives were turned upside down. I replayed memories of long walks up to the farmers' market, pushing Shola in her stroller, to buy the best produce for her baby-led weaning.

While I'm blessed to finally taste motherhood after a battle with infertility, those precious early years were drowned out by the volume of a spinal cord injury that commanded my full attention. The grief that I won't have those days back stings.

I spent a good 20 minutes holding on to that steamer, memories activating, tears flowing, as I wondered if I still really needed it after surviving for five years without it.

Somehow I just didn't want to let it go.

We often hold on to things because of insecure attachments, fear of loss, scarcity mindset, or a lack of trust in the future. We can struggle to let go because items can feel like sources of comfort, control, or security, even when they no longer serve us. This is when they might end up acting as anchors to past versions of ourselves, old memories, or unfulfilled hopes.

We need to ask ourselves: 'Is the memory in my heart and mind, or is it really in this item?

Furthermore, does this item serve me now and represent the direction of my growth? Is it aligned with who I'm becoming?'

If it doesn't reflect the life you're stepping into, it may be time to release it.

If you're struggling to part with something, consider taking a photograph of it as a visual keepsake before letting it go. This allows you to honor the memory without holding on to unnecessary physical clutter.

To ease the process, you can have a designated memory box or two, where you can keep things you definitely want to hold on to, but you might find it helpful to put a limit on the number of boxes! For items you're unsure about, have a holding box or a specific space where you temporarily place them for review at a later date.

Giving yourself permission to let go gradually can help soften the emotional resistance and build your trust in the process.

You may find, over time, that the need to hold on to certain things recedes. This is a sign of growth and progress.

While I personally didn't feel entirely ready to face the boxes of our past life, confronting them helped me release the cloudy sense of the unknown that was lingering oppressively in the rafters.

Facing the murky can bring us clarity and empowerment as we consciously assess and bring order to our surroundings.

The Art of Energetic Housekeeping

Ritualizing your decluttering process can transform a mundane task into an intentional act of release and renewal. It can help clear stagnant energy, elevate your vibration, and untangle emotional and energetic attachments.

Through the art of energetic housekeeping, we can also create a deeper connection to our space. This intentional process supports us energetically and provides a nourishing foundation for activating our light. It nourishes and inspires the soul to expand beyond the energetic limitations prescribed by outdated versions of ourselves.

LIGHT ACTIVATION

Energetic Housekeeping

Spend some time reconnecting with your space, bringing intention to how you view the different areas of your home.

- Ask yourself, 'How do I feel at home?'
- Consider what your space might be communicating about your inner world. Move through each room, cupboard, and drawer, feeling into the energy of the objects around you.

- Notice which areas are calling to you. Is it your overcrowded wardrobe, loft space, or kitchen drawer? Which stagnant spaces are calling for your attention?

Once you identify an area or space for housekeeping, you can begin the process of releasing what no longer serves you.

1. Set Your Intention

- Before you begin, take a breath.
- Anchor in an intention that resonates with you. You can create your own or use this one:

'I set the intention to release with ease,
accept with grace, and liberate myself in
the name of my healing and evolution.'

Let this intention gently guide you as you cleanse your space physically and energetically.

2. Declutter

Review your physical space and any clutter in your digital space. Notice which items feel heavy, purposeless, or unaligned with your evolving direction.

- Throughout this process, feel into your body's first response. Is it an expansion or contraction? With an expansion, you find yourself beaming, feeling light, inspired, and open as positive feelings and emotions open you up energetically. In contrast, you may find items that make you contract and cause you to tense up as you become impacted by negative energies or your thoughts that turn to events from the past that feel unsupportive to your wellbeing. Or it could be that you're simply uninspired by an item. Notice the subtle changes to your state when assessing what needs to go.

- If you feel called to do so, play music that supports your emotional or energetic release. Whether it's something to stimulate your tears and move you through emotions or something that brings higher-vibe energy to help you raise your vibration, trust that you know what your soul needs.

- Give yourself permission to move slowly and intentionally. Ideally, it's not a process to be rushed.

- Not everything needs to be thrown away. Consider what feels good to you. You can:

  - organize and file
  - sell
  - donate
  - recycle
  - gift

Some things just feel super sticky, even when you know, deep down, their time with you has come to an end. Letting go isn't just about clearing space, it's an act of energetic hygiene.

When you pass something on to a friend, a charity, or its next rightful place, clear any lingering energetic ties so you can truly let go and the item can move on without attachments.

- Speak resonant affirmations over your space, such as:

> *'With love and gratitude, I release all that no longer serves me, making space for what uplifts my soul.'*

'My home is a sanctuary of clarity, light,
high-vibe energies, and abundant blessings.'

- Before you release the item, hold it and take a few deep breaths to ground yourself in the present moment. Ask yourself:
  - 'What has this item come to represent?'
  - 'What deeper emotional connection does it carry?'
  - 'Why am I holding on to this?'
  - 'What am I afraid to release?'
  - 'Does it still serve me?'
  - 'How will I feel once I let it go?'

As you hold it, notice what thoughts, memories, and emotions arise. Acknowledge any feelings of grief or guilt, or any attachment issues that arise as you consider letting it go.

Be present with whatever emerges.

- Now, bless the item with gratitude. Out loud or in your mind, thank it for the memories, lessons, and experiences it has carried. Send it love as you prepare to let it go, knowing that with its release, you're creating space for new, aligned energy to flow in.

That might be enough, but if you still feel deep resistance:

- Close your eyes and ask your body: 'Where is the energetic cord to this item located within me?'
- Trust the first thought, image, or sensation that comes.
- Visualize the cord, its attachment to you, its texture, thickness, and color.

- Imagine holding a pair of scissors in your hand. When you're ready, gently cut the cord.
- Take a breath in, and with a long, slow exhale, feel the energetic tie dissolve.

Feel the spaciousness expand within and around you. Breathe into this renewal, knowing that with each release, you make space for new blessings, ones aligned with who you're becoming.

3. Cleanse the Space Physically and Energetically

Once you've cleared your physical space, it's time to shift any lingering energetic residue:

- Open the windows to invite in fresh air and circulate new energy.
- Dust and mop in rarely touched corners where stagnant energy tends to settle.
- If you feel called to smoke cleansing, consider working with local herbs and woods that align with your culture and personal resonance. Rosemary and cedar are effective cleansers. If burning herbs, always do so safely, catching embers in a fireproof container. Be mindful that smudging with white sage is a sacred Indigenous practice. Honoring it means understanding its origins, acknowledging the historical persecution of Indigenous communities, and approaching it with respect over entitlement. Empower your ancestry and reconnect with alternative cleansing methods that feel authentic to your own lineage and spiritual path, if necessary. It will strengthen your light.
- If smoke cleansing isn't for you, try a cleansing spray with essential oils like sage, juniper berry, lemon, or pine, and uplift the space with lavender, frankincense, myrrh, or eucalyptus.

- Even without herbs or sprays, intention alone is a powerful force. Use breath and visualization to move energy through your space and release it through an open window.

When cleansing or making sprays, hold the intention of releasing stagnant energy and uplifting your space with high-vibrational frequencies. Approaching this practice with intention allows you to honor the process and work in harmony with the energies that are present toward your objective.

4. Rebuild Your Energetic Space with Intention

Now that you've cleared out the old, you can be the mindful architect of how you build the energy of the space up.

- Bring in plants to nurture and refresh the energy.
- Ethically sourced crystals can help to raise the vibration of your home.
- Add flowers for beauty and vibrancy, with gratitude to the plant.
- Choose natural-based candles with essential oils instead of synthetic fragrances to minimize environmental toxins.

Your space should feel like an energetic sanctuary and a reflection of your highest self. Breathe it in. Feel the shift. And bask in the heightened vibrations you've nurtured.

This process isn't just about what you release, it's about what you invite in. By letting go of the physical and energetic weight of the past, you create room for your light to grow and align your home with your highest potential.

....

LIGHTWORK

Life Audit

So many of us, over time, compromise our truth, our needs, and our personal values by unconsciously following societal ideals of what life should look like: the so-called stability of a nine-to-five job, a mortgage, 2.4 children, and the latest car or designer clothes. But what truly matters to you when you dissolve these societal 'shoulds'? What is it that you genuinely value?

By examining the following five key areas of your life, you can illuminate aspects that might be stifling your growth and dimming your light.

By bringing mindful awareness into these areas, you can then begin to make adjustments that pave the way for more aligned energy to flow into your life.

Find a quiet and comfortable place where you can connect with yourself. Light a candle, bring your favorite form of hydration, and grab your journal and a pen.

The aim here is to openly express your heart and mind, without self-censoring. You don't need all the answers or solutions right now, just to surrender to the flow of what wants to emerge.

Set the intention to allow your truth to unfold onto the page.

Bring light to the following areas:

1. Work and Purpose

Reflect on your current job or life's work.

- What aspects of your work bring you joy and fulfilment? What drains your energy?
- Even if you're not sure about your life's purpose yet, think about what activities make you feel alive and spark the inner light of your true self.
- If you aren't in alignment with this in your work yet, do you know why?
- Are there fears or limiting beliefs that are holding you back from pursuing your true calling?
- Are there external pressures or expectations that are influencing your career choices?
- How can you move closer to work that feels meaningful and true to who you are?

2. Relationships and Connection

Examine your relationships with family, friends, and community.

- Which relationships uplift and inspire you? Which feel toxic or unsupportive?
- Are there unresolved issues or dynamics that need your attention?
- Are there repeating patterns in your relationships? What might these be trying to teach you about yourself?
- Are you avoiding vulnerability or difficult conversations? Why?
- How can you nurture deeper, more meaningful connections with the people in your life?

3. Self-Care and Wellness

Assess your physical, mental, and emotional wellbeing.

- How well are you taking care of yourself?
- Do you have practices that nourish your body, mind, and soul?
- Do you notice any patterns playing out that mean you don't prioritize your own self-care?
- Are there underlying beliefs about self-worth that might be affecting your self-care routines?
- Are you using any unhealthy coping mechanisms to deal with stress or emotions? If so, think about why.
- What changes could you make to improve your overall sense of wellness and vitality?

4. Personal Growth and Spirituality

Reflect on your journey of personal development and spiritual growth.

- What practices help you connect with your inner self?
- Do you feel disconnected from your spiritual path? What might be causing this disconnection?
- Are there any fears or resistance that come up when you think about deepening your spiritual practice?
- Are there past experiences or traumas that are stifling your spiritual growth?
- What new areas of learning and growth are calling to your soul?
- How can you nurture a deeper sense of inner peace?

5. Environment and Home

Consider your living space and its impact on your energy and wellbeing.

- How does your environment support or hinder your growth?
- Does your living environment reflect your inner self?
- Are there external factors, like location or financial constraints, that impact your living space?
- Visualize your ideal home sanctuary and what steps are needed to create it.
- What changes could make your home space more nurturing and harmonious?

6. Core Values

After reflecting on each section, take some time to discern your core values.

- Write down what you value most in life. These are the principles and beliefs that guide your actions and decision-making.
- Reflect on how each area of your life aligns or conflicts with these values.

7. Integration

- Think of at least one action that you can take in each of these key areas to help you bring all the areas of your life into better alignment with your core values.
- Take the defined action steps to set the energy in motion.

PART II

Activate

Awaken · Ascend · Activate

Awaken your soul energy and connect to your light.

CHAPTER 6

Shine from Your Heart Space

'Follow the call of your heart. It's led by the wisdom of your soul.'

After doing the mental and emotional work to move out of our heads, we'll begin to deepen the activation of our light by bringing awareness to our energetic essence.

Let's begin here with our energetic heart.

A Divine Instrument

Many of us have long been in the habit of over-identifying with the noise of the mind, leading us to miss out on the rich connection and soul guidance the heart offers. The heart is a divine instrument that plays its frequency out into the universe. When it's open and clear of stagnant debris, it becomes a powerful magnet that easily attracts love in all its forms, aligning people and opportunities with ease.

And when we consciously tune in to it, it speaks in subtle sensations and impressions of knowing that act in favor of our highest good, supporting us in amplifying our essence and bringing us online to our magnetism.

When we follow our heart's subtle calls to action, our energy expands as we develop a trust in the wisdom that, time and time again, allows life to exceed our expectations.

But, like any instrument, the heart needs to be tuned, because its sweet song is distorted when it's weighed down by fear or past pain. This frequency distortion can attract experiences and situations that aren't in tune with our highest outcomes. Instead, these outcomes will create a sense of unease, and if we pay attention, they'll allow us to examine the instrument a little more closely to see what's causing it to play so out of tune.

When you attune your heart to its pure resonance, life harmonizes with you.

This is when you won't need to chase what's meant for you. It'll flow to you, drawn by the music of your soul.

This isn't just some romantic, poetic sentiment. It's an energetic reality.

Interestingly, many of us rarely think of ourselves as energetic beings. If we can't see something with our physical eyes, we tend to ignore or dismiss it. But energy is always present and plays a big part in the natural world and in our human experience.

If this feels like a far-fetched concept, think about it this way: In your day-to-day life, without seeing it, you trust the invisible forces of Wi-Fi to connect to the internet, Bluetooth to connect your earpods, and electricity to power your home. You don't doubt their existence because you experience their effects in your life. Still, because of our conditioning, many of us overlook and find it hard to trust the unseen energy within ourselves.

Can you think of a time when you walked into a room and immediately felt the vibe was off before a word was spoken? Maybe you met someone whose presence sucked all the good vibes out of the room. Or the opposite happened, and you met someone whose energy felt warm and magnetic without even having a conversation with them.

You didn't need science to tell you that energy was there; you knew it was because you felt it.

Science has revealed, however, that the heart is the most powerful energetic force in the human body. The HeartMath Institute has shown that its electromagnetic field is 60 times greater in amplitude than the brain's, and its magnetic field is over 100 times stronger, extending three feet beyond the body.[1]

This means that your heart isn't just beating physically in your chest. It's also an energetic powerhouse. A frequency generator. A living, beating transmitter of vibes.

It's an energetic force that influences the world beyond your physical form. It leads the silent, energetic conversation that's happening all the time, setting the tone for the dialogue you're having with the universe around you.

The Heart Connection

When we begin to work consciously with our heart and detach from the noise of our mind, we start to remember who we truly are and why we came here. Through this remembering, we send out stronger, clearer, and more confident signals from our heart,

---

1. McCraty, R. (2015), *Science of the Heart, Vol II: Exploring the Role of the Heart in Human Performance; An Overview of Research Conducted by the HeartMath Institute*: HeartMath, Chapter 6

which start to draw toward us all that's meant for our growth and enjoyment.

However, standing between us and a shining, activated heart is often the calcified, stagnant residue of past heartbreak and pain that has dimmed our heart's light. This heaviness often comes from previous disappointments and a gradual descent into mistrust, stemming from past hurt.

Maybe you can count many ways in which your heart has been hardened or conditioned into mistrust over the years?

Have you ever looked at your life – the pain, the struggle, the endless disappointments – and started to feel foolish for ever thinking that things could work in your favor? Or even convinced yourself that your little life here on Earth was just to be one of suffering? Perhaps, after a barrage of bad luck, you stopped expecting much at all.

The challenges may have been so relentless that daring to believe in something better felt naïve, almost delusional. Perhaps you adjusted accordingly and learned to lower your expectations, not because your heart wasn't calling for more, but because hope had started to feel like a risk you couldn't afford to take.

And so it became a matter of protecting your heart at all costs.

But while you may have learned to disconnect from your heart, your heart has never stopped whispering, waiting to be heard, gently reminding you of your soul's essence and your real potential.

The heart is where the finite meets the infinite. It's the gateway from the body to the most ancient, conscious self, the soul. If spirit is the divine life-giving energetic force that flows through all things, weaving its way through every atom, particle, and corner of this eternal existence, then I feel the soul is an individualized aspect of that divine web. It's your eternal non-physical essence that holds the memory of past wisdom and future possibilities.

You can think of your soul as the Big Momma or Big Poppa of your energetic existence; the older, wiser, all-knowing presence that carries the blueprint of who you really are. The you that existed before the world told you who to be. The you that is free and uninhibited by the limitations and perceived imperfections of the physical body or the programming of this life.

And then, there's your human self, like the child, the curious one who absorbs life through experience, learning through trial and error.

Like a dutiful parent, your soul has already set you up for the most expansive and abundant life possible, but like any good parent, it can't control your every move. So, it steps back and lets you live, make your own choices, and use your free will.

Like any loving parent, the soul is, however, always observing. While it won't interfere, it often sends signals and warnings through intuitive nudges, gut feelings, other bodily sensations, and inner knowings.

The question is: Are you paying attention?

Just like a child who ignores their parents' warnings not to touch the hot stove, sometimes, despite our soul's best efforts, we don't listen to our intuition and we do it anyway. And when we do, we often get burned.

As the old Caribbean proverb goes, 'If you can't hear, you must feel.' That's why you're beginning your activation process here, with your heart energy, so you can clear the way and reconnect with your intuition.

Your heart is a divine compass that wants to help you follow the yellow brick road to your highest timeline. And the more you nurture that connection, the clearer the signposts become. Through healing your heart, your intuition will be strengthened, your soul's whispers will be received with pronounced clarity, and you'll deepen your sense of discernment so that you can begin to trust more, open more, and expand your heart energy to receive more.

How the Heart Speaks

The heart speaks loudly through the things that make us contract in resistance and the things that open us up in love. It's the dreamy, satiating frequency of heart-expanding divine love that serves as a powerful manifestation magnet, the energy that harmonizes our divine instrument with the truth of what lights us up.

You can feel the expansion of your heart energy when you connect with people you love and the things that light up your soul, when you express your creativity or listen to music that moves you, when you experience the wonder and beauty of nature and the vast, starry night sky that reminds you how infinite and expansive you really are.

When you heal and reclaim the parts of yourself you had to shut down so you could survive and when you reconnect with your intuition and activate that divine spark within, your energetic field shifts. Finally, you stop playing small.

For many, this reconnection to the heart brings them back to their scintillating, multidimensional essence.

When you begin to open to the power of the heart, you begin to feel your way through life instead of forcing it. You stop chasing. You start attracting. Synchronicities become clearer. Intuitive nudges become louder. And you begin to see evidence that your heart has been trying to guide you all along.

So, pause for a moment.

Take a breath.

Celebrate yourself, my friend. It takes a fierce kind of courage to trust, soften, and surrender. Celebrate your willingness to confront the shadows that have kept you from your light.

Our patriarchal society has conditioned us to dismiss our heart intelligence as romantic and impractical, and those who choose to follow their heart are considered daydreaming fools, as if following its whispers will lead to inevitable disaster.

But what if that has never been true...? What if the heart has always been the clearest channel to the soul's truth, one so powerful that the structures of global control depend on us staying disconnected from it?

When you awaken to the intelligence of your heart, you begin to see with great clarity. You begin to question everything about your place within this existence. You start recognizing the ways you've been conditioned to ignore your own knowing and accept limitations that were never yours to begin with.

If all of humanity were to reclaim this power, if we all operated from the expansive force of the heart, the systems that exploit, manipulate, and keep us small and divided could no longer be upheld.

The heart is a force of liberation.

What Causes the Heart to Harden?

To really sink into the softening of our heart, we need to be aware of how a heart becomes hardened in the first place and how a hardened heart might manifest.

You may sense within yourself that a protective crust has formed around your energetic heart as a self-preservation mechanism, fortified by life's painful moments.

That self-preservation mechanism may manifest in that once-bitten, twice-shy energy where you perpetually keep your guard up.

Or is it in the quiet, sneering bitterness that continually sees the worst in everyone and everything? Is it a lingering sense of suspicion that causes you to narrow your eyes and keep others at arm's length because you can't bring yourself to trust fully?

Or maybe it's the part of you that holds fiercely on to grudges, staying unforgiving because forgiveness feels like letting someone who caused you pain off the hook.

From the outside, looking in, it might even look like arrogance, but deep down, that's just another way to shield your vulnerability.

It may manifest in a defensiveness that automatically resists and pushes back.

Or maybe it presents as a numbness and shows up in you being unmoved, uninspired, or disconnected from the things that once lit you up.

In my encounters with others who are healing their heart, I've found that much of what caused them to harden in the first place was rooted in trust that was freely given but ultimately betrayed.

At some point, we all feel betrayed in one way or another by love, friends, family, or life itself. And it's in those painful moments that our sense of trust is shaken.

We trusted someone with our heart, and they mishandled it.

We trusted that if we worked hard, things would fall into place, but they didn't.

We trusted that love would last, but it ended.

We trusted that if we showed up fully as ourselves, we would be accepted, but we were judged or rejected.

We trusted that if we were kind and good, life would be kind to us in return, but it was not.

And so, we adjusted our expectations and told ourselves that trusting was a mistake. We became determined that no one or anything would do us wrong again. And a determined layer of self-protection formed around our tender heart.

It often starts subtly, presenting as a little more hesitation before opening up. Perhaps a little more suspicion before trusting someone's intentions. You might find your sense of hope fades away, to be replaced by a cynicism that causes you to energetically brace yourself for less favorable outcomes.

And one day you come to realize you're not just protecting yourself from pain, you're blocking yourself from experiencing the great potential that life has to offer.

The Invitation to Soften

Take a breath.

Consider how your heart might be constrained by the energy-restricting patterns created by past wounds. Can you sense how these mechanisms have imprisoned your heart's energy behind protective walls?

When we close our heart, we think we're protecting ourselves, but it's like keeping a bird covered and caged when it has the wings to fly and experience the vast beauty of the world.

I wonder what it would feel like to uncover the cage of your heart, open the door, and let the light in again.

I invite you to pause here.

- If it feels safe, close your eyes, just for a moment.
- Imagine what it would feel like to allow your heart to soften and expand again, and to trust that in its softening, you're safe and returning home to your essence.
- Take a deep breath into your heart.
- Notice how your ribs create space for its opening, like that bird-cage opening up.
- As you exhale, allow yourself to release a satisfying sigh as you surrender to the presence of your heart.
- I recommend scheduling an intimate date with yourself to begin the process of reconnecting with your heart. Block out the time in your calendar and bring into your sacred space your journal and things that make you feel safe and comfortable. Close the door, put on 'Do not disturb,' and let your date begin.

- You might have first-date anticipation. I recommend that you come without the expectation of any fixed outcomes and just arrive with a willingness to connect.
- If your mind's noisy or your nervous system resists slowing down, know it's normal. Softening can feel unfamiliar, especially if you've been in survival mode for a long time.
- Sitting quietly, bring your awareness to your breath.
- If your mind's busy, you might want to do a busy brain download (*see p.34*) and write out everything that's circling in your head.
- If resistance comes up, notice it. Be with it. You might even want to journal about what's coming up for you.
- Then return to your breath.
- Repeat three times one of the following or any other affirmation that helps bring you inner ease:

'I am relaxed.'

'I am safe.'

- Let your awareness drop down from your mind into your heart space, beneath your breastbone. You might find it helpful to visualize a warm golden light starting at the top of your head and melting down to gently pool in your heart space.
- If it feels good, place your left hand over your heart and your right hand over your left, or simply feel your attention resting there.
- Breathe into this space.
- Set the intention to listen to your heart.

- Ask yourself:

  'What am I ready to release so I can respond from love instead of fear?'

  'How can I allow the greatest expression of my heart to expand?'

- Now, think of a time when you felt amazing. Fully alive, radiant, at peace. What made you feel that way? What did it really mean to you? Who were you in that moment? Did you feel confident, powerful, loved, authentic, inspired? What was the spark that lit you up?
- Notice how this memory feels in your body. Pay attention to how your energy shifts and how your heart space expands when you reconnect with that version of yourself. How does it feel?

....

My heart's healing is an ongoing journey. I'm still peeling back the protective layers, learning to surrender more deeply into trust, and noticing the ways in which my nervous system has yet to fully exhale into safety.

And, of course, it hasn't.

My body has been conditioned in mistrust. Perhaps yours has, too?

From the moment I lost G, to the relationship that followed, the one that showed me all the ways love could cruelly wound me if I dared to open my heart again, to the various traumas my physical body experienced over the years, from sepsis to a hemorrhage, the spinal cord injury that changed my life, and now a fibromyalgia diagnosis, a very real physical manifestation of what happens when the body is locked in perpetual distrust at a cellular level, I learned that the world could turn upside down at any moment.

My body had been in survival mode for so long that trusting, like *really* trusting, felt dangerous. I was sure that if I let go too much, something would inevitably go wrong.

But in order to heal, that's exactly what I needed to do: relax into trust.

I needed to soften the hardness around my heart. I had to be willing to be vulnerable in a way that my entire being fiercely resisted.

In my previous relationship, my kindness was taken for weakness, my heart was abused, and I learned the hard way that not everyone will honor you with the respect you deserve. I was betrayed by a person who knew the depths of my loss, who listened to stories about my pain, yet still chose to exploit my broken heart while it was raw and healing.

I was enraged by his disrespect and learned that to be seen, I had to scream.

But even in my rage, I wasn't heard.

When Kane and I first got together, I had to put in the work to be willing to stay open enough for life to show me something different and prove to me that positive outcomes, love, kindness, and safety were all still possible.

And Kane held space beautifully for that to happen. He became a protector of my peace, not a provocateur of my pain. He was different and became a mirror for me to see the ways that life had hardened me. He became the permission slip for me to let down my defences and start slowly allowing my heart to soften again.

For the first time in a long while, I didn't need to scream to be seen, because Kane just listened.

And bit by bit, something in me began to shift.

My heart began to open like petals stretching toward the sun after a long, dark winter, and as I let myself soften and trust, the whispers of my heart grew stronger and stronger.

As I began to open, I was reminded of the rumbles from my soul that said I deserved more. Here it was, manifesting beautifully for me in real time, reminding me of what could happen when I listened to those intuitive nudges that I'd suppressed and overridden for so long.

As the walls around my heart slowly lowered and I gradually let down my guard and embraced a new way of being, my nervous system had to adapt. It was time to release the expectation of conflict and welcome the calmer, more peaceful, and more joyful way of life that was unfolding.

The noise slowly quietened. Like the tide going out, the crashing waves of life's drama receded.

The whispers of my potential held in my heart had been patiently waiting to be heard. Like a diamond lost in the ocean, glistening from the depths of the seabed, they became more visible once the relentless tides had eased their grip.

That's the thing about a hardened heart: it keeps us from seeing beyond the limits of our wounds. It traps us in old stories, convinced that what has been is all that can ever be.

But a softened heart?

A softened heart makes room for our highest timeline to emerge.

Healing the Heart

Healing the heart is a process. It's often not quick, but it's something to be worked on and nurtured. It can begin with some gentle self-inquiry and by slowing down and dropping into the heart space.

Self-Inquiry Journal Prompts

What activates your heart? Ask yourself:

~ What lights me up?

~ What causes my heart to harden?

~ What does my heart want for me?

~ What's holding me back from trusting my heart?

~ What's my heart longing to express?

~ What needs to be cleared so I can hear the messages of my heart more clearly?

For a daily check-in, you can also give yourself at least five minutes to simply sit with your heart and listen to what it has to say, using either of these prompts:

~ What does my heart want me to know today?

~ What does my soul wisdom want to share with me today?

You might like to alternate between these questions or intuitively choose the one that resonates more in the moment.

There's no need to force any answers. Simply hold the space. Some days, insights can pop into your mind in the form of words or sentences, or as feelings, intuitive nudges, knowings, bodily sensations, or visions, and on other days, there may be silence. That's okay. Take the pressure off yourself. The key here is that you're giving your heart an opportunity to speak, and that in itself is a form of healing.

Take a breath.

There are also other ways to create a deeper connection with your heart. You could make a vision board or digital collage of all the things that light you up and open your heart, and come back to it often for a heart-expanding boost. Try listening to music that stirs something deep inside you and create a playlist of songs that activate your spirit.

Bit by bit, day by day, by reconnecting to your heart, you're creating more opportunities and space for your inner light to shine. The heart speaks in feeling, sensation, and energy. When you give it room to be heard, it'll begin to show you the way forward.

LIGHT ACTIVATION

Nurturing Your Heart

Now that you've started the healing and reconnection process of activating the light of your heart, you can begin nurturing and reintegrating previously closed-off parts of it.

- Find a quiet, still moment and settle down somewhere you won't be disturbed.

- Take a breath and visualize deep roots anchoring you to Mother Earth.
- Remember, you're the keeper of this heart in this lifetime and you're blessed with the great honor of helping it restore its luminosity.
- See this heart recovery as an act of great service to yourself, your inner child, and your future self.
- Take a moment to step outside yourself and observe your heart from the outside looking in. What do you see? Does it appear dusty, calcified, heavy, or dim? Simply witness it without judgment.
- Now, let us begin the cleansing process. What tool comes to you for this clearing? A soft cloth, a large feather? Perhaps you feel called to simply blow any debris away. What feels good for you?
- Imagine gently clearing away any debris and brushing off any dust that's formed over time.
- If your heart feels calcified in a tough exterior, visualize holding a crystal-infused spray in your hand. What color is the crystal in the spray? Trust the first image that comes to you.
- With each gentle spritz, you'll find the deposits begin dissolving at the point of contact. Old pain, past trauma, and protective walls soften and release their hold.
- Take a deep breath. Exhale slowly.
- Notice how your breath flows with more ease and how the energy of your heart begins to expand outward.
- Take a moment to mentally reconnect with the energetic fragments of yourself exiled for protection and survival, the

parts that were too radiant, powerful, and full of life to risk being dimmed. They exist across time and space, waiting to return.

- With the power of your intention, call them back home now, with the words:

> *'I call all fragments of my energy*
> *back to their powerful center.'*

- See them traveling through space and time, drawn back to you like golden threads of light.
- As they return, they are purified, alchemized, and reintegrated into your being.
- Watch as your heart begins to glow, radiating a brilliant golden light. With every breath, this light expands, filling your entire body and surrounding you in a luminous, magnetic field of high-vibrational energy.
- Take a breath. Drink it in. Feel the shift.
- Stay here for a moment.
- Let yourself shine.

....

CHAPTER 7

Illuminate with Gratitude

'When you open your heart to gratitude, you harmonize with magical realms of possibility, inviting blessings into your orbit, magnetized by your devotion to what is already enough.'

Gratitude is the queen of queens when it comes to activating your heart energy. We're talking about more than just a polite thank you; it's the kind of gratitude that makes you shine at an energetic level – an embodied sense of gratitude that shifts your frequency and brings you in closer alignment with the abundance that is present around you.

If I were to define it, I'd say:

> **Gratitude** (ˈgratɪˌtjuːd) *noun*
> A deep soul-level appreciation for the blessings, lessons, and everyday magic woven into our existence.

When you look through a lens of gratitude, it impacts your spirit. You don't just elevate your mood, you raise your whole vibration, activating your light and aligning yourself with the magic of life itself.

Raising Your Vibration Through Gratitude

In the last chapter, we explored the heart as a divine instrument, a bridge between our physical and non-physical aspects. Gratitude is a powerful way to tune this instrument.

Gratitude is a practice, and I say 'practice' because it isn't just a feeling that shows up when life's easy and things are working out in our favor. It's something we need to actively practice when the chips are down, so we don't free-fall into the lower echelons of our vibration and stay there.

Imagine yourself as an energetic piano. Every thought, every emotion, is a note. What kind of tune are you playing?

You can spend your life repeating the low, heavy notes of fear, guilt, and self-doubt. Or you can start exploring the higher notes, the frequencies of joy, love, and gratitude.

When you learn to master your instrument, you begin to master your energy. The more you practice gratitude, the more you fine-tune your vibration and shift into harmony with the life your soul knows you came here to create.

On the scale of human emotions, gratitude vibrates at a high frequency, sitting close to love and joy. These are the emotions that expand our energy, open us up, and connect us to higher states of being. They are the energies that lift us up, magnetize more good into our lives, and keep us flowing in alignment with our highest potential.

On the flip side, emotions like guilt, fear, and shame weigh us down and keep us stuck in lower-vibrational patterns that disconnect us from our true power.

But just as we've formed low-vibe patterns through our life experiences, as we explored in previous chapters, we also have the ability to reprogram ourselves to operate from higher-vibe patterns of being. Focusing on gratitude naturally makes these patterns easier to access and maintain.

Gratitude isn't about pretending things are perfect. It's about shifting our awareness to what's already good, and the moments of beauty we might otherwise overlook.

It's a tool that helps us find balance in our hardships and on our bad days. It's about recognizing the blessings and the lessons encased within the mundane, and even within the challenges.

In our energetic conversation with the universe, gratitude's a powerful way of saying, 'I see and appreciate the blessings in my life.' It shows that we can perceive the beauty already present, so when more blessings arrive, we're able to recognize them as such.

Granted, blessings aren't always instantly recognizable, but even our most difficult times can contain a gift. This isn't toxic positivity. We're not bypassing our hardships, which is why we're also working with those in this book.

Opening my heart to gratitude is one of the greatest life skills I've learned, and it's helped me to find beauty in life even on the most challenging days.

If you try it, you, too, might find beauty in hidden places. If someone once wronged you in a relationship, perhaps you'll come to give thanks, not for the pain itself, but for the strength it gave you to leave, rise, and become more of who you were meant to be. And perhaps for the ways it pushed you forward, even when you didn't feel ready to move yourself. Because sometimes, the things that break us down are the very things that are sent to realign us with our higher soul path.

Gratitude's about realizing that perhaps the closed door was protection, the betrayal a redirection, and the detour a reroute to the path that would lead you to your highest life.

It's in the moments that you got through, when you thought you wouldn't.

It's the song that found you at the right time to bring you healing.

The kindness of a stranger who brought connection when you needed it most.

The breath in your lungs, the sun on your face, and the simple fact that you're still here.

There's still more for you to receive, more for you to give.

Maybe, just maybe, there's even more to be grateful for than you might perceive right now.

When we choose to shift our focus away from the 'Why me?' mindset and the misfortune of the less-than-ideal circumstances we've faced, we stop feeding our sense of internalized victimhood with our energy. From this empowering space, we can deepen what it means to take radical ownership of our experience and begin to turn our gaze toward what we can be grateful for.

Gratitude gives us a fertile foundation from which to rise.

In a soil enriched with gratitude, we can plant magnificent seeds, and the universe adds its magic, bringing the right conditions for them to take root, grow, and flourish.

So often we get caught up in what's missing from our lives, and all that isn't so good. We focus on what we don't have and what hasn't happened yet, and without even realizing it, we're communicating that energy into the universe.

Lack, lack, lack.

As mentioned earlier, though, gratitude isn't about forcing yourself to be positive when you don't feel it, it's about retraining your awareness to see the blessings that already surround you.

A Hard-Earned Lesson in Gratitude

It's not always easy to access gratitude when life keeps knocking you down, when you're stuck in a job you can't stand, or when you're grieving a loss that leaves a deep ache in your heart. When your body isn't working as it used to, or you feel unseen, unheard, or disrespected.

In those moments, it can be difficult to feel grateful.

You try. You go through the motions, but you just don't feel the feels.

I know because I've been there too.

The concept of gratitude and its impact on life was first introduced to me through *The Secret*, the film that later became a #1 *New York Times* bestselling book by Rhonda Byrne. This was my entry point into manifestation and the Law of Attraction, and it was the first time I began to understand gratitude not just as an acknowledgment but as a powerful force that shapes our reality.

Back in 2007, my homegirl Tali lent me and my bestie Collette a copy of *The Secret* movie. It was as if we'd stumbled upon some hidden formula that could magically transform our lives and bring us all the riches we could ever dream of.

Dr Bob Proctor told us that our inner world, our thoughts, beliefs, and emotions shaped our outer reality. That was my first awakening to the impact of the inner world on the outer world.

We were also told that one of the ways to get what we desired was through gratitude. That to attract more wealth and abundance, we must first become more grateful.

This was a revolutionary idea for me. Later, I came to realize that knowledge can only ever really meet you where you're at. And at the time, I had a very simplistic idea of what gratitude was.

But, with my newly found understanding of this universal law, I was ready to put my basic knowledge of the Law of Attraction to the test.

At the time, I hadn't long moved to London. Moving from my cozy and familiar world of Birmingham to the bright lights of the capital city was a baptism of fire. When I lived in Birmingham, I'd drive to the office or get a lift with my friend Hardeep. Now, I was stressed out and crammed into public transport like a sardine in a tin.

On my commute from Stamford Hill to Liverpool Street station every day, before getting on the train, I'd pick up a copy of the free *Metro* newspaper to distract myself from the anxiety, homesickness, and low-level grief that coexisted through all seasons following G's death.

One day, I spotted a competition. They were giving away a Mini Cooper. Now, before this, I had zero desire for a Mini Cooper. I was perfectly happy with my 10-year-old little blue 1.1L Volkswagen Polo.

But having just learned the magical secrets of manifestation from *The Secret*, I was convinced that if I entered, I'd win.

So, I entered.

They said in *The Secret*, 'Feel it as if it's already yours.' I tried my best. Every morning, I'd stare at that newspaper clipping of the Mini, force a smile, and repeat to myself, 'I am so happy and grateful to be the winner of this brand-new Mini Cooper.'

But I wasn't happy. And I definitely wasn't feeling grateful. I was just forcing a feeling and thinking that fake smiling at a bit of cut-out newspaper would trick the universe into delivering me a car.

The big day came. The competition was closing. I waited for the call.

But it never came.

What d'you mean I didn't win?! I thought I was manifesting it! So much for The Secret, I thought.

What I didn't understand at the time was that gratitude isn't something you can fake your way through. It isn't just empty words spoken through gritted teeth. The universe speaks in vibration, so if you're faking the funk, the vibes won't be genuine.

I was definitely faking the funk.

I was focused on the lack in my life while trying to force gratitude, simmering in stress and self-criticism.

I was completely unaware of my own energetic state.

I spent my days scurrying around London, overwhelmed, carrying several suitcases of unprocessed emotions and, let's be real, the only thing I was magnetizing was more stress, impatient people on my commute, and manspreaders to sit next to on the train.

A new car? LOL.

I was trying to manifest an arbitrary material desire from a very low vibration. At the time, I didn't see how it was all connected. I had no idea what it meant to actually *embody* gratitude. My understanding has most definitely evolved with my life experience.

How many of us focus on manifesting random material desires that we think we want and need, and use them as the benchmark for whether our life is successful and worthy of gratitude or not?

When Life Changes in a Moment

Fast-forward 13 years from when I first discovered *The Secret*, to February 2020, when I would be served a hard lesson in discovering a deeper kind of gratitude that was patiently waiting to be acknowledged all along.

We were just days from my daughter's first birthday party. After a long infertility journey, my husband and I were excited to celebrate this milestone occasion with a few special people, but I'd been in excruciating pain with a bad back and sciatica, or so I thought. The pain was out of the ordinary, so I booked an appointment with my GP.

After a tearful visit, seemingly unable to perceive the true extent of my pain, my unconcerned doctor sent me home with a prescription for some painkillers and a number to call to self-refer for physio.

Nothing to worry about, or so I was made to believe.

The night before the birthday party, the outside of my right foot started to go numb. In the morning, I booked a last-minute appointment with an osteopath, hoping they would perform some kind of magic that would help get me through party day, but the gentle manipulation during the session only made things worse. The searing pain had now spread to both my legs, and I was just about ready to pass out.

When I arrived home from the appointment and went to step out of the cab, I couldn't feel my legs.

I remember that despite being scared that I was paralyzed, at that moment I felt relieved that I couldn't feel the pain anymore.

An hour before the party was due to start, an ambulance took Kane and me to the hospital while my parents took my daughter to her party. Guests would be arriving from all over London. It was too late to cancel.

Confident they'd give me some medication to fix it and I'd be back cutting the birthday cake in a few hours, I'd no idea how serious things were about to get.

An MRI scan revealed an alarming picture. This was a medical emergency. Cauda equina syndrome.

A herniated disc was crushing the bottom of my spinal cord, specifically the cauda equina bundle of nerves responsible for sending and receiving messages to and from the lower limbs, bladder, bowel, and genitals.

The doctor explained the risks. If they didn't operate immediately, I'd be permanently paralyzed and lose function in all those areas, and even if they did operate, there was still a chance of paralysis. There was also a risk of death associated with surgery.

My eyes were wide with bewilderment as he handed me a waiver to sign before we could continue with the surgery. My hand trembled as I took the pen.

Terrified, I was wheeled immediately to the anesthetist. He tried to lighten the mood by asking about my daughter and talking about kids' TV shows like *Bluey* and *Daniel Tiger*, but it didn't help, as my mind was gripped by thoughts that I might possibly never wake up to see my loved ones again. I tried to resist the anesthetic, fighting the pull into the dark abyss of the medication.

I was out for five hours while neurosurgeons fought to save my bodily functions.

When I woke up, the first thing I said was, 'I'm alive! I need to phone Kane.'

The days that followed were humbling. I lay in a hospital bed, drainage tubes in my spine, a catheter emptying my bladder, and an unforgiving wound stapled together on my lower back. I couldn't move without pain. I couldn't walk. I couldn't hold my daughter, and my breastfeeding journey ended there. I was forced to stop nursing her due to the amount of medication I needed to take. I was heavy with morphine-infused milk that soaked my hospital gown, and after such a long fertility battle, this all felt so cruel.

One minute, I'd been moving into our new family home and planning my daughter's first birthday. The next, I was naked in a wheelchair, being bathed by a young nurse, as I sat in my own grief, feeling my dignity wash down the drain along with the hot, soapy water.

What have I done to deserve this?
was the ever-present thought.

The Gratitude Shift

Two weeks after I was discharged from the neurology ward, the country entered lockdown. No home visits. No inpatient rehab. No follow-ups. The world and my support systems were locked down. It was just me, my husband, my baby, and my broken body, alone in a third-floor flat in a global pandemic.

One morning in the days that followed, I was sitting on my bed getting changed when I caught a glimpse of myself in the mirror, body bruised and spirit dented.

Holding a catheter bag filled with my urine, I grieved not just for the body I'd lost but the life I'd had. I grieved for the years I'd wasted hating my body, punishing it for not living up to some impossible European beauty standard. Since secondary school, I'd internally annihilated myself for not having a 'perfect' body. I used to curse my Lipodema legs every time I caught a glimpse of them.

There are 57 steps to our flat, and I came so close to never being able to climb them again. And yet those legs, those 'big, fat, ugly' legs that I'd spent a lifetime cussing, they still showed up for me, despite the trauma of this injury, and slowly but surely, they got me back into our flat.

'Thank you,' I whispered quietly, as I looked at my legs, 'thank you.'

I was being given another chance to fix up and to start being grateful.

Tears streamed down my face. Something shifted that day. I started to feel truly grateful. Grateful for all the things I'd previously taken for granted.

I saw a body that had been through hell but still showed up for me. The body I'd spent years tearing down had grown me a baby after infertility. It had pulled me through sepsis and hemorrhage during labor, and now spinal cord injury. I saw its loyalty to my survival.

Despite how cruelly I'd spoken to it, despite the shame, the judgment, the blame, it was still there. Still showing up for me.

Like, wow, Zo. Your body has really overcome some tough stuff.

As the days passed post-injury, spring crept in and my feelings of gratitude continued to expand. Housebound, I found myself bringing my mobility chair up to the kitchen window, eager to make some connection with the outside world. Every time my daughter napped, I sat quietly and watched the trees as the bare branches slowly began to bud and the new leaves unfurled in the warming sun.

In the stillness, nature began to communicate to me of its own resilience, of how the seasons changed and how, after a long, dark winter, the sun returned and trees and plants began to bloom again.

I felt so much gratitude for these small reminders that even in the darkness of my inner winter and grief, I would bloom again in the right season.

With this emerging sense of gratitude, I felt guided to start listing all the ways I felt blessed by life and the things I was grateful for, like the trees outside my window, the simple warmth of the sun on my face, and the birds and their song, and how they all reminded me that I was a cell in a bigger picture of the natural world, which all moved on. I felt blessed that I was able to return to my home, a privilege not afforded to everyone with a spinal cord injury. I felt deep gratitude for my husband, who supported me through the unimaginable darkness and transition into disability. I felt blessed to have a family that had offered me unconditional love and support through all of life's challenges. I felt grateful to have food in my cupboards and clothes on my back. And particularly blessed to have a baby daughter who inspired me to get up and do my very best every day, because she was watching.

For the first time, gratitude wasn't something I forced with a fake smile. It was something I felt. Something I embodied. Not to get anything in return. Not to manifest a new car or a comfortable material life. Simply because it felt so deeply honest, and in expressing it, I was rooted into the beauty of the present moment like I'd never been before.

Instead of looking to acquire material things in life, I could see the true, nourishing fulfillment within the simplicity of life and the natural world in its most basic and natural form.

From this connected place, my emotional and physical pain seemed to be reduced into insignificance.

In this truly grateful state, I found my true peace.

This true gratitude naturally aligned me with a higher frequency of existence. It helped me to see new layers of truth that had previously been obscured. The material illusion of our capitalist consumer conditioning disintegrated, the illusion of material satisfaction subsided, and I saw that true fulfilment can be found without the frills and price tags. I awakened to a deeper level of spiritual truth that helped me find gratitude everywhere I looked, raised my vibration, and shifted how I saw my life and the world.

With my heart rooted in gratitude, blessings appeared with ease.

The more I found to be grateful for, the more I aligned with things to be grateful for. Now, I entered competitions and seemed to win time and time again, winning everything from a year's supply of hair products to a full year of eyebrow threading at a high-end salon to luxury hampers filled with beauty products, even a dishwasher, just when I needed one.

I started to align with the right mentors, who appeared at the right time to guide me to new levels of my potential. Opportunities arrived that expanded my world and grew my network.

But in addition to all of that, the real manifestation of my truly grateful heart was the woman I was becoming, the woman who no longer saw herself as cursed or a victim of life but as so highly blessed in many ways.

I became the one who no longer asked, 'Why me?' but instead whispered, 'Thank you.'

So many of us perpetually focus on what's not going right and what's less than perfect and forget to show gratitude for all the blessings that are already under our nose, like Veruca Salt in *Charlie and the Chocolate Factory*, who stomps her feet, entitled, and demanding more without a moment of gratitude for what she's already had.

Let's be a little less Veruca and a lot more Charlie.

Embodying a Grateful Way of Being

Once you truly embody gratitude, your entire perspective on life shifts. What if you were to become committed to evidencing all the ways that life did work for you? What if you saw the blessings and tiny miracles that popped up around you, even in less-than-ideal situations? What if you shifted your gaze to see all the beautiful ways in which you were indeed blessed?

It can take some work to change your habits, but once you do and you begin to see the impact that making these changes has on your life, commitment to this way of being becomes easy.

Let the magnetism of a grateful vibration give you all the evidence you need to make this a way of life.

What if you did the Mirror Work exercise (*see p.64*) and scanned yourself from head to toe to feel unconditional gratitude for all the parts of yourself, just as they were?

What if you felt gratitude for the roof over your head?

What if you took a moment before each meal to feel the blessing of having food to eat? Or someone to eat with. What if you took a moment to give thanks to the farmer who grew your produce and to nature for providing the conditions for it to grow?

What if you gave thanks to the sun for the warmth and light it brought and thanks to the rain for the way it replenished life on Earth?

Then gave thanks for the trees, plants, and insects for their contribution to this ecosystem of life.

Or at the end of the day, as you slipped into bed, you gave thanks for the safety of your home and a place to rest your head.

Or each time you drank a glass of water, you held it for a moment and acknowledged its gift. What if you gave thanks for the hydration, the healing, and the life it gave your body? What if you were to bless it? In turn it would bless you.

If gratitude feels hard to grasp, imagine, just for a moment, what life would be like without these things, not to dwell on lack but to deepen your appreciation for their presence.

Do you see all the ways you are blessed? You are blessed, you are blessed, you are blessed.

Gratitude elevates even the simplest of day-to-day duties into sacred moments.

If you viewed life as a gift, how might that change the way you lived your days?

Without bypassing pain, can you, right now, hold space for the full complexity of your experience? Can you allow gratitude to coexist with challenges? Can you seek the richness, the depth, and the hidden blessings rooted in your difficulties?

That's not to say the hardship itself is a blessing, but can you hold space to explore the wisdom, strength, or transformation that may emerge from it?

Self-Inquiry Journal Prompts

How do your past experiences shape your ability to feel grateful? Ask yourself:

- ~ Am I focusing more on what I lack than what I have?
- ~ When I think about gratitude, is my focus on material things?
- ~ Am I comparing my life to those of others in ways that makes gratitude difficult?
- ~ Do I dismiss small blessings or take them for granted?

The richness of experiencing life as a gift to be revered allows each day to unfold as a miracle of infinite possibilities.

LIGHT ACTIVATION

Gratitude Practice

I invite you to commit to a gratitude practice for the next seven days. This practice will help you expand your awareness and attune yourself to your blessings. It's about deepening your ability to notice and appreciate what's already present, allowing gratitude to become a natural part of your way of being.

1. Daily Practice: The Gratitude List

Each day, write down 10 things you're grateful for.

These can be big or small. Something that makes you smile, a moment of connection, an act of kindness, the beauty of nature, or simply the feeling of being alive.

As you write each one down, take the time to pause, breathe, and connect to the feeling of gratitude.

- Why does this matter to you?
- How does it make you feel?

Allow gratitude to settle in. Notice how it feels in your body, your heart, and your breath.

2. Deepening Your Gratitude Practice

This next step invites you to deepen your practice by truly feeling gratitude as an energy within you.

- Find a quiet place where you won't be disturbed. Sit comfortably, close your eyes, and place your hand over your heart.
- Take a deep breath into your belly and slowly exhale, allowing yourself to settle into stillness.
- Bring into mind something you're grateful for. Choose something that stirs a deep, grateful feeling within, whether that's a person, a particular moment, a feeling, or an experience that makes your heart expand.
- How does this gratitude feel in your body? Where do you notice it most? Is it in your chest, stomach, womb, hands, or somewhere else?
- If this feeling of gratitude had a color or energy, what would it look like to you?
- What deeper meaning does this feeling represent for you? What does it awaken within you? A sense of love? Safety? Connection? Belonging? Something else?
- With each inhale, imagine gratitude as a light in your heart space. See it growing, glowing, warming, radiating outward.
- With each exhale, let it expand beyond your chest, filling your entire being.
- Let the energy of gratitude move through you. Does it feel like warmth spreading through you, an inner sparkle, a gentle expansion, or a sense of deep peace? Allow yourself to fully experience the sensation. Breathe into it.

- As it moves through you, feel it dissolving tension, softening resistance, and grounding you fully in this moment.
- Rest here. Absorb it. Receive it.
- When you're ready, gently bring your awareness back to the present moment and take this expanded sense of gratitude with you as you move through your day.

3. End-of-Week Reflection

At the end of the seven days, take some time to sit with your journal and reflect.

- Has your awareness of the blessings in your life expanded?
- Did you find yourself noticing gratitude more easily as the days went on?
- How has this practice shifted your perspective, even in subtle ways?

Let this practice be a foundation to build on to support you in allowing gratitude to move through your spirit and days in deeper and more meaningful ways.

CHAPTER 8

Your Altar of Light

'Your altar of light is a womb of potential, a sacred space where the divine and the human meet to cocreate, a place where magic is birthed. With every intention, every flame lit, every breath and healing tear, you evoke the potential of this energetic space.'

What if there were a dedicated space where your physical self and your soul self could assemble with the high-vibe energies of the universe at a magical meeting-point right in your home? An altar of light where healing deepens, intentions amplify, and the practice of gratitude opens a clear channel to the unseen realms. A dedicated space for you to deepen your roots and grow your light.

An altar of light can become a powerful portal for energetic nourishment, spiritual growth, and deeper connection. Think of it as a power hub for your prayers, healing, manifestation, self-reflection, and soul evolution.

This is a place for you to build your spiritual connection in a way that feels authentic and true to you. Whether you feel called to connect with God/Source, your ancestors, guides in spirit, or your highest self, your altar can reflect your beliefs and deepest connections.

But don't worry, you don't need to get caught up in labels. Instead, focus on your intentions and the energy you want to create, perhaps for healing, deepening your spiritual practice, connecting with your guides, honoring your ancestors, manifesting your dreams, or simply coming back home to yourself. It could be a space for grieving, for gratitude, for clarity, or for remembering your worth.

When you're in the process of activating and maintaining your light, your altar can help you to build a regular practice of sitting in the energy of devotion and possibility. It's a living, energetic entity that will grow and evolve with you through life's seasons.

It can help bring you into deeper connection, not only with yourself but also the unseen realms. It becomes a bridge to accessing the enriching higher dimensions that are available to support your path.

In this fast-paced world, your altar can also become a space for stillness and deep, soul connection. It serves well as a place for you to recalibrate, reconnect, and anchor in your energy amid the hustle and bustle of daily life.

It's a perfect place for letting your human self rest in the energetic arms of the Divine.

An Energetic Cauldron

An altar needn't be fancy. It can be a shelf, a corner, a table, or part of your desk. But whatever you choose, when you create an altar it symbolizes a deeper commitment to your soul-led path.

The Light Activation at the end of the chapter will take you through the process of creating your altar; for now, know that it's an intentional space where you can grow your magic and cocreate with our energetic universe.

You bring all the right ingredients, as you would for a Dutch pot, but with the intention of creating something nourishing for your soul. Your altar becomes a sacred cooking pot, perhaps even an energetic cauldron, where you contribute your intentions, gratitude, and vibes.

You can include anything that helps you feel powerful, grounded, connected, and spiritually activated. Let it be a reflection of your light.

You don't need to gather everything at once; allow it to build and evolve over time. Here are some ideas to inspire you:

- things from the natural world: flowers, crystals, stones, leaves, shells, wood, water
- photos/pictures: ancestors, loved ones, guides, people who inspire you
- spiritual items: candles, incense, oils, oracle cards, deities aligned with your cultural or spiritual beliefs
- sentimental things: ancestral items, jewelry, notes, symbols, anything that carries the right energy for your intentions and empowerment
- a journal for inspired writing, reflection, and soul inquiry

When I set up my altar initially, I was simply following my inner guidance to create a space that I could come to for my inner work, to sit still, and focus. It started off with books, plants, and journals, and evolved over time as more power objects came into my life.

Now I have white candles, crystals, oracle decks, books, plants, essential oils that I use to create healing sprays, and other items that uplift, inspire, empower, and hold deep meaning for me.

One such item is a beautiful jewel-encrusted golden crown, gifted to me by my friend Madeline McQueen, executive coach, speaker, and founder of the Brilliance Summit. Madeline hosts powerful events, and at one of her Christmas Me4Me gatherings for Black and mixed-Black women in leadership, she gifted each of us a crown to remind us of how precious we were and to encourage us to walk with our heads held high, without shrinking. She wanted us to remember our worth and our value, and the crown is a powerful symbol of that.

One thing about Madeline: she won't just leave you feeling that you can take on the world and succeed, she'll leave you knowing that you can, knowing that you're worthy, and that you're more than enough. So that crown sits on my altar as a powerful reminder of all of that.

I also have a special birthday card that was drawn for me by my friend, illustrator Ruth Davis of Ogna Proggle. On the card she drew the trees outside my window, the very trees that held me through my healing during the pandemic, and she included the robin redbreast who is a regular visitor to their branches. Robins hold a deep, spiritual significance for me. On my altar, Ruth's card represents connection, creativity, and friendship.

For my 40th birthday, my dear friend Farah Orths, author of *Money Loves Me*, gave me a stunning goddess ornament imprinted with the maiden-mother-crone symbol. To me, it represents the divine feminine, sisterhood, and the rich seasons of being a woman.

I acquired another power item during a visit to the Hay House office on the day I was offered my publishing deal. My commissioning editor, Kezia, invited me to pick a card from their big glass bowl of oracle cards. The card I pulled was Lemuria from Rebecca Campbell's *Work Your Light* deck. As I pulled it out and looked at it, I had goosebumps. I've had a deep curiosity about and connection to Lemuria since it revealed itself to my consciousness in powerful and synchronistic ways throughout my spiritual awakening. The message on the card read: 'Creating heaven on Earth. It's happening.' That card now sits on my altar as a sacred reminder of the greater mission behind all of this: the healing we're here to spark, and the role we each play in creating a more awakened and light-filled world.

On the altar, I also have herb bundles for smoke cleansing, drawings from my daughter, a photo of one of my spirit guides, my late grandmother Theresa, and a white feather that landed on my arm as I was visiting my grandad Norm's grave, along with other personal trinkets.

I add current intentions, prayers, and visions, and recharge the tools I use in healing sessions. Anything that touches this space is blessed with love, filled with light, and drenched in healing. The altar is a space for magic to happen.

Power, Prayer, and Insight

When activated with intention, your altar impacts the energy of your entire space. Think of it as a charging dock to energize your connection, energy, dreams, and evolution.

You might come to your altar to give thanks, ask for clarity, write, cry, meditate, receive insight, or celebrate your wins and manifestations. You might come to honor your ancestors, anchor a vision, or to simply sit in the stillness and listen. You might feel called to journal, to move your body, or to just be.

Your altar meets you where you are.

Having this dedicated space is especially powerful when you're moving through a healing journey or a spiritual awakening. The practice of coming into gentle stillness there can help you regulate your nervous system and bring you into deeper presence.

It becomes a place where you can sow the seeds of new high-vibe practices so they can take root in your way of being.

When you come to your altar, treat it as a sacred time. Step away from the distractions, put your phone on 'Do not disturb,' and reconnect to your breath, your body, and your intention.

Being in ritual with your altar of light brings you powerfully into the present moment, creating a potent point of focused energy. Your altar becomes a place of energetic possibility, a space for both offering and receiving.

Come to it when you need clarity, comfort, courage, or connection. Light a candle, pull a card, write in your journal, be still, listen, cry, celebrate, ask, and give thanks.

The more present you are within the energy of this space, the more powerful and enriching the offering.

Don't come with rigid expectations, come with gratitude, openness, and a willingness to observe the subtle.

Here, you might experience spontaneous emotional releases, waves of joy, or profound downloads, or you can deepen your self-inquiry and tune in to the wisdom of your body. You can ask what your body needs from you or if there's a way it needs you to move to help facilitate healing or to shift energetic blocks. You might find that you're guided into a deep stretch or a gentle roll or rotation of your limbs or joints.

When you sit in your sacred space, you might find that you're intuitively drawn to connect with a specific item from your altar, to hold it and quietly connect to its frequency. If this happens, you can gently observe any messages, intuitive prompts, or feelings that pop up, or you might even find yourself called to start journaling.

Some days, you'll receive sparks of inspiration. You might find yourself awash with an energy that inspires you to write page after page without stopping, or you might hear a single word or observe a symbol that lands in your mind's eye.

Keep your journal close and make a note of all the threads that flourish in this space. Even if at the time they seem random or insignificant, you might just find down the line that they become part of a breadcrumb trail leading you deeper down your higher soul path.

At my altar, on my healing journey, I'd find old energies that had been forming blocks in my energy field would emerge for review and release. Moments from the past would pop up in my awareness, almost like bubbles with a little projector inside that would show me mini-movie clips of moments from my life, each bringing its own frequency. Some bubbles contained memories of simple but joyful moments in nature as a child or other nostalgic memories, and others carried memories that provoked tears that needed to be released, but it wasn't as if I was being dragged into the pain of the memory, just its essence. Energetic shifts came with streaming tears, but I wasn't forced into the pit of my pain. It was as if the stagnant energy was moving through the tears to be released in the most healing and therapeutic of ways.

Other times, I'd sit with projects or ideas and ruminate for a while. When the time was right, clarity and downloads would stream through, sharp, energized, and clear.

Sometimes, I'd go there to sit and I'd hear names in my head, see symbols that I couldn't quite decipher, or be given random songs that contained a message or an energy to which I could connect.

I knew I was being guided in the most loving and empowering way by forces far greater than myself in ways that were beyond my comprehension.

The altar became my favorite place for divine collaboration. A place where the channel was so clear and the guidance so rich, supportive, and love-filled that returning to it often was the only thing that made sense. It became a way of life. Not in an obsessive or expectant way, like 'I'm showing up at 9:45 and the divine energies had better deliver,' but more like 'Let me show up for the greater good today and trust it will unfold exactly as it's meant to under that intention.'

When you commit to showing up in the name of the greater good, the energies that serve that same mission assemble to support that goal. It doesn't always look how you might want it to or expect it to, so it's best to show up with a pure intention and surrender any expectations.

In my experience, expectations are often a fast track to disappointment.

Working with Your Altar of Light

If you're feeling that now's the time to begin creating your own altar, the Light Activation at the end of this chapter will guide you through it.

It isn't just about setting up an aesthetic space, it's about curating a sacred energetic container for your light to grow.

Setting Your Intention

Setting your intention for your altar is important. Build it in your vision with pure focus. You want it to be a high-vibe place of light, guided by love, and aligned with the greater good of all. When created with loving intention, an altar is a space so energetically protected, it becomes impenetrable to anything not aligned with love and light.

An Act of Service

In many ways, this is more than a personal ritual. When we come to our altar with a high intention, we're contributing our light to the wider grid of collective consciousness and to the healing and light of the world.

So, bring your projects, visions, and ideas to your altar and ask for them to be infused with the frequencies of light that will support the highest possible outcome, not just for you but for humanity.

Let this be a space where inspiration flows in service to something greater. Magic happens when we move beyond self and into service.

Altar of Light Rituals

You can do any of these daily, weekly, or monthly:

- Light a candle and sit in silence while you observe the flame, without expectation, simply being still, and softly observing.
- Lay offerings at your altar. These can be physical, such as candles or power items, seasonal offerings like flowers or herbs,

or energetic offerings through spoken words and held intentions, like gratitude or prayer.

- Pull an oracle card for guidance, and before rushing to read the interpretation in the guidebook, notice or write down any message that comes through regarding what it means to you and how it relates to your life. This will help you fine-tune your intuition. (I love working with Sophie Bashford's *Goddesses, Gods & Guardians* deck.)
- Try a burning release ritual:
  - Write patterns, habits, or fears that you're ready to let go of on small bits of paper.
  - Add some salt to a heatproof bowl of water.
  - Light the paper over the bowl.
  - Drop the embers in the water, and when you're finished, offer it back to the earth, giving it what no longer serves you.
- Or a salt-spray ritual:
  - Fill a spray bottle with salt water.
  - Bring what needs to be released into your awareness.
  - Spritz your aura with the salt water, holding the intention to dissolve and transmute any stuck energy.
- Journal at your altar for deep, soul inquiry.

....

Let's keep it real, you can do any of these rituals anywhere. But there's something uniquely powerful about returning to a space you've carefully nurtured with heart and intention.

Remember, though, that showing up at your altar isn't about perfection or strict rituals that leave you feeling guilty if you don't visit when the demands of life get on top of you. Life happens. Give yourself grace.

Word to the Wise

An altar of light is a sacred space for healing, alignment, and higher guidance. It's not designed for dabbling with lower-vibrational energies. Of course, you have free will to do as you please, but just know that spiritual work is powerful, and with that power comes responsibility.

If your intention is impure or driven by ego, you open yourself up to entanglements that can distort the energy you're creating, and you may invite in what you don't want to receive. So, do so at your own risk. This isn't to fear-monger, this is to empower you.

For example, if someone's wronged you, it can be tempting to want to seek vengeance, but rather than bringing their name to your altar for spiritual retribution, consider setting the intention for your healing and for them to be drenched in divine light so potent that it illuminates their harmful patterns and supports their awakening. That isn't weakness, it's spiritual mastery. We're in the business of growing our light and our potential, not lowering ourselves to someone else's shadow.

Be a force of light in a world that desperately needs it.

Cleansing Your Altar

You'll want to keep your altar clean, both physically and energetically. Clear away dust regularly and to maintain the space's energetic hygiene, you can use tools like bells, chimes, herbs, incense, or resin smoke.

An altar can act like a mirror, so if you've been stressed, overwhelmed, or out of sync and your altar's gathered a little dust, that's okay, we're imperfect busy humans after all, but let that be a gentle point of reflection for you to notice if you do need to slow down, realign, shift out of an energetic funk, and reconnect.

A great way to reset is to come to your altar with the intention of cleaning the space and the items. As you reconnect to clean and cleanse, you might also visualize clearing off the energetic dust from not only the altar but also from yourself.

Take time to clear out anything that no longer feels energetically aligned with this season of your life. It doesn't mean those items can't be returned later, but take the time to check in with each one consciously. Ask yourself, 'Is this still serving the vibration of this space?' If the energy has dwindled, it may also be asking you to check in with yourself, to question, 'Where am I right now? What do I need in this moment?'

Self-Inquiry Journal Prompts

Consider your altar, with these questions:

~ What does this altar want me to bring to this space to be healed?

~ What am I being asked to remember about who I really am?

~ Who am I becoming?

~ What is my soul trying to whisper to me in this season?

~ What energy am I ready to embody more fully?

An altar becomes a living reflection of your devotion to your light, a portal that responds to your presence. The more love, reverence, and energy you offer it, the more clearly the wisdom flows.

Less noise.

More truth.

Deeper connection.

And now, if your heart feels ready, let's begin creating your very own altar of light.

LIGHT ACTIVATION

Creating Your Altar

It's time to create your altar, a sacred space to remember who you are, where you're going, and the magic that lives within and all around you. This is your power portal, a reflection of your spirit, a space to hold your intentions, energy, prayers, and magic.

1. **What Are Your Intentions for This Space?**

- Whatever intuitively rises for you, trust it.
- And know that whatever your intention may be, at its core it's always about bringing you back to your light. To your truth and that divine spark within.

2. **Allocate a Space**

- Remember, an altar can be a shelf, a corner, a table, or part of your desk. It can be as big or as small as you want or need it to be. This isn't about ticking boxes, it's about working with what you have and where you're at.

3. Collect Items That Resonate with Your Intention

- Be guided by your intuition. You don't need to go out and buy anything fancy. The most powerful objects are often the ones that already hold meaning for you.
- Let every item hold a purpose. Your intuition will guide you.
- When your altar is set, if you have one available, light a candle to symbolize the introduction of light to the space. If not, no worries.
- Take a breath. Feel into the space.
- If they resonate, say these words aloud, or feel free to tweak them or create your very own:

'I create this altar as a portal of love and light,
a sacred space for my healing, connection, and soul growth.
May this altar hold my intentions, amplify my energy, and
connect me with divine guidance.
May this space evolve with me
and always remind me of who I truly am.
So it is.'

Congratulations on creating your power hub of possibilities, my friend. May the seeds of light sown here manifest in beautiful and magical ways.

CHAPTER 9

Support from the Energetic Realms

'Self-healing and creating a deep connection to ourselves and the subtle energies of the universe around us is the quiet revolution our world is truly waiting for.'

Let's start with a breath. Through that rich, nourishing inhale, do you notice how your ribcage expands to take in more of life? Like the rib cage on the inhale, your awakening energy field is expanding. It's stretching beyond the restrictions of the mind, beyond your small sense of self, and into the vast, magnificent energetics of infinite possibility.

When you rise above the density of your earthly struggles and attune to the fine magic of the high-vibe energetics around us, you clear the way to connect to the guidance and love that have been surrounding you all along.

The volume of our energetically noisy world and the interference of our dysregulated nervous system can place a heavy demand on our subtle senses.

If you were being stung by a swarm of bees, would you hear someone gently whispering, 'I love you'? Probably not. You'd most likely be in fight or flight and facing the crisis.

That's how I often see our relationship with our energetic guides: We're so focused on life's problems that we miss the quiet, loving whispers from the subtle realms that are calling out to be noticed.

In this chapter, we're opening up to receive the light that's already reaching out to connect with us. We'll invite in the supportive, higher-vibrational energies that reside in the realms of spirit to illuminate our path and guide us toward the highest expression of our lives.

Whoever you resonate with, be it God, source, creator, spirit guides, ancestors, angels, ascended masters, your higher self, inner wisdom, or all of the above, this chapter will help you deepen your relationship with the higher guidance that's there to lovingly support you on your path.

Opening to Guidance

Your guides are there to help you fall in love with life's true wonder and magic. To gently support you as you begin to imagine and create a future far more expansive than the one a carefully conditioned mind had you believing was possible.

This is about allowing yourself to believe that your most audacious life is possible and trusting that your guides will help illuminate the way.

A wealth of wisdom and potential exists across the energetic web of existence that spans dimensions beyond which our common human senses are conditioned to perceive. We've been led to believe only in what we see or what can be justified scientifically. But we do know from science that energy never dies, it simply changes form. So, just imagine the conscious energy that exists out there within our collective energetic field.

We're more interconnected, powerful, and perceptive than we've been led to believe.

Some people find themselves naturally receptive to psychic information, but it's not just a privilege reserved for the 'gifted few.' I believe we all hold the potential to connect to the subtle in our own ways.

Through doing the inner work to clear out stagnant noise, we're attuning ourselves and creating ripe conditions to become more effective receivers of wisdom from spirit. As we develop a sense of spaciousness, we allow the guidance to land.

Do you remember the old-school style radios with the manual tuner? If you weren't tuned in to a specific frequency, you'd be picking up all the white noise and static in between. Can you recall how, when you fine-tuned the dial to the right frequency, you could pick up your favorite radio station loud and clear?

That's how it is with our energetic guides. They exist on a different frequency, like another channel on the radio, and to connect with them we have to create the right conditions within ourselves, adjusting our frequency to receive. We can do this by doing the healing work and creating opportunities to be present and clear in intention.

Then, just like adjusting our radio dial, we begin to pick up the messages, insights, and guidance that have been broadcasting all along, waiting for us to tune in and hear them.

Resistance to Connection

As you prepare to deepen your connection and open up your communication, you may find some resistance or deconditioning that needs to be addressed before you can fully reconnect with the simple, beautiful truth of having a relationship with your guides.

Before I started my healing journey, one of the UK's leading psychics noticed my intuitive abilities. They gave me homework and a simple practice and invited me to go home and connect with my spirit guides. If I developed, there was the potential for a job offer.

But honestly? I was so scared.

As a child, I was psychically sensitive. I had a lot of experiences with energy, and some were high-vibe and loving, and some were definitely on the lower-vibe end of the spectrum. It left me feeling confused and alone, because no one around me seemed to see, feel, or hear what I did. I didn't have the language to explain it, and no one could help me make sense of it. On top of that, the religious narrative many of us grew up around carried the message that anything outside of 'God' must be demonic, so I stuffed down my fear and confusion, slept next to a mini-Bible and a bottle of holy water, and hoped it would all go away.

Between the fear in my body as a child and the fear passed down through the culture around me, I carried the resistance into adulthood.

So when it came to doing the psychic's homework, it was a big fat 'hell to the no' from me and my nervous system, which wasn't at all at ease with the idea of sitting down to meet any kind of spirits.

And let me tell you, Hollywood also has a lot to answer for. Movies would have you believe that a full-sized apparition will appear at the end of your bed in the still of the night, or your late Uncle Bob will come floating through the wall with a message from beyond the veil.

I wasn't ready for any of that.

But in reality, based on my research, my lived experience, and my observations of those I guide, connection with spirit is less of a full-blown cinematic event and more of a subtle experience for most of us.

The Language of Guidance, Signs, and the Subtle

It's so subtle, it can easily be missed if we're not present enough to notice. It's in that gentle shift of energy that nudges us to look up at exactly the right moment and catch the sign. Perhaps you've been called to look up and see those numbers like 222 or 11:11 that show up like little winks from the universe.

Maybe you've seen a robin that's always sort of been there, but now a loved one has passed away, it has a deeper meaning, and it somehow embodies their energy every time you see it.

Maybe you're somewhere and a car drives past, blasting a song with a lyric that jumps out at you like a direct message to your soul.

Or you observe a change in resonance in something that's typically average, but the deepening weight in its energy piques your curiosity, and invites you to follow the call to explore.

Be present and give yourself the room to notice the changes. Give yourself some space in the morning, before you reach for your phone and start absorbing everyone else's thoughts and energy. Instead, allow your dreams to breathe a little longer so you can receive their messages and wisdom before opening the floodgates to the world.

The connection may show up as a pull toward a particular city or place that you can't quite explain, but when you follow it, you meet your soulmate.

Or maybe it's the unexpected invitation that lands you in the room, space, or place where everything changes, the room you didn't even know existed before, but somehow your soul knew what it needed to do to get you there.

Sometimes, guidance tells you to go out and meet the world; other times, it calls you to stay home and rest.

It might nudge you to lean in to a new connection.

It might also let you know that it's time to step back, and in doing so, you sidestep a future drama, like dodging the snake in a game of Snakes and Ladders.

This is how our inner knowing and our guides work with us, lovingly steering us toward what's in alignment with our highest good by weighting everyday things with an added touch of energetic magic.

We're like the counters on a board game, making our next move one step at a time. And our guides are like the ones who have the whole board in view. They know the shortcuts, the detours, the ladders we're meant to climb to elevate us through the game, and the places where we might go backward if we don't listen. Each path brings its own set of lessons.

When you choose to tune in, you gain access to a bigger perspective and start to move differently, with more purpose, grace, and trust.

And the game of life?

It becomes richer, so much richer.

And you feel held. So deeply held.

You come to find joy in the mundane and possibility where there was once fear.

But to truly receive this enrichment, you have to meet it from a place of healing and self-awareness.

If you try to expand without doing the inner work, you can easily mistake fear, trauma, and old wounds for truth. You might hear the lower-vibe energetic interference of your past fears and limitations instead of the wisdom of your soul and guides.

Sometimes guidance will stretch you as it pulls you toward growth and calls you to step beyond the familiar confines of your comfort zone. It can feel uncomfortable, but it should never feel dangerous or harmful. Through your healing and discernment, you'll begin to recognize the difference. You'll know when it's an old limitation speaking, a part from the past that wants to keep you small, safe, and stuck.

That's why you've been working to heal, clear the static, and raise your vibration. When your energy's clear, you become finely tuned, so you can discern the difference between an old fear and an encouraging energetic nudge.

Deep in your field, you'll feel, with a 'whole-spirit yes,' what's really in service to your highest path.

There's something so healing and empowering about connecting to greater, wiser energies.

When you catch the glimmers, the sparks of light, the loving evidence of something greater, and you begin to sense the vastness of this experience, the true magic, and your rightful place within it, the carefully constructed societal illusion of limitation begins to dissolve, freeing you from the smallness you've been taught to live inside and returning you to the expansive truth of who you really are.

A Gentle Note on Mental Wellbeing

As we open more fully to the unseen realms and start recognizing how the universe communicates with us, it's not uncommon to question our sanity, especially when our experiences fall outside the boundaries of what society has taught us to expect.

If you ever feel overwhelmed, hear harmful or frightening voices, or struggle to distinguish between intuitive guidance and distressing thoughts, please seek support from a trusted professional.

Your spiritual connection should feel loving, grounding, and empowering, not confusing, chaotic, or unsafe. Your high-vibe guides will never speak through fear. Their guidance will always be clear, resonant, loving, rooted, and expansive.

We're all born with an inner antenna designed to help us connect with these unseen currents of wisdom, love, and guidance, and we'll explore these now.

Receiving Guidance Through Your Intuitive Senses

Our intuitive senses are part of who we are, built into the very essence of our being, but somewhere along the way, we were taught to narrow our perception and only trust our five traditional senses – taste, touch, sight, hearing, and smell – as if these were the only valid ways of experiencing reality. As if everything that mattered was tangible, measurable, and explainable.

This idea keeps us disconnected from the truth of our power.

Your intuitive senses, commonly called your 'sixth sense' or clair senses (*clair* meaning 'clear' in French), are just as real and powerful as your other five. Whether you're conscious of them or not, the chances are that you've already experienced them.

Understanding how our clair senses might manifest in our life helps us expand our understanding of them so that we can work more effectively with them.

Introducing the clairs...

Clairvoyance (Clear Seeing)

Seeing beyond the physical realm through your inner vision.

It can show up as:

- seeing pictures, symbols, or scenes in your mind's eye
- experiencing psychic visions or flashes of insight
- noticing sparks of light, energy fields, or auras around plants, animals, and people
- having vivid, visually detailed dreams or past-life memories
- seeing visual metaphors or symbolic imagery
- catching glimpses of movement or light in your peripheral vision
- seeing orbs, flashes, or colors
- blinking to refocus after seeing something out of the ordinary

Clairaudience (Clear Hearing)

Hearing beyond the physical realm.

It can manifest in various ways, including:

- hearing song lyrics or the names of songs unexpectedly within your mind
- experiencing an inner hearing of phrases and names
- perceiving whispers or spoken messages in the sleep/wake state
- detecting high-frequency shifts or high-pitched noises that are distinct from tinnitus
- hearing messages in your own internal voice or a voice that feels separate from yours
- being sensitive to loud sounds and high volumes, due to the energetic sensitivity of your ears

Clairsentience (Clear Feeling)

Feeling subtle energies and emotional vibrations within your own body.

It can show up as:

- feeling subtle shifts in energy, atmosphere, or vibration around you
- picking up on the emotions of others even before they express them
- deeply sensing and sometimes absorbing other people's feelings as if they were your own

- experiencing physical sensations in your body that correlate with intuitive information, such as goosebumps or chills, tightness, warmth, or softening
- feeling an instant 'yes' or 'no' in response to people, places, or decisions without logical explanation

Claircognisance (Clear Knowing)

Knowing information without a logical explanation.

It can present as:

- experiencing sudden inner truths or insights that feel deeply certain
- having a strong sense of knowing something is right or wrong without needing external proof
- receiving flashes of ideas and information that are later validated
- meeting someone and instinctively knowing they'll play a significant role in your life
- feeling a deep certainty that lands in your body, even when your mind can't explain it

Some people also experience a connection through smell or taste, like catching a whiff of your grandad's cooking or your granny's favorite perfume when no one's around, or tasting something that brings up a message from the past.

Do any of those clair senses speak to you? Do any stand out like, *Yes! I've experienced that!*

More and more of us are coming back online to our spiritual selves, and these experiences will only increase as we move out of the density and stagnant energies of the past, creating space for higher-vibrational, faster-moving energies to flow through.

Following the Guidance

I could write a whole book on the multitude of ways my guides have shown up for me, but one story in particular sums up the magic, the synchronicity, the non-linear and multidimensional nature of this cocreative relationship and how it led me deeper into the world of energy healing.

It began after my spinal cord injury, after I'd been broken open at every level – mental, spiritual, and physical. In the months after my injury, I started receiving very profound guided meditations that landed clairvoyantly. It was as if they were coming through me, but not from me. I'd close my eyes and a meditation would form in my mind's eye, unfolding step by step. All I needed to do was follow it, and it would facilitate powerful healing, deep emotional release, and activation.

I started sharing these practices with others, and they, too, began experiencing profound shifts that helped them move beyond attachments, past trauma, and blocks. I share some of these activations with you in this book.

One day, while I was sitting quietly at my altar, I was guided inward into meditation and taken to a golden temple. It was beautiful. I saw floor-to-ceiling stained-glass windows with a bright, soothing angelic light flooding through the vibrant colors in the glass. I was led to a large stone bath filled with water. I felt that I was being cleansed and healed as I lay there in the vision, bathing in the water and light. It was so rich and nourishing, and the colors seemed to penetrate every particle of my physical and spiritual being. I was awash with a deep sense of peace.

In the middle of my meditation, I randomly peeked open one eye. To my absolute amazement, floating above my altar was what I can only describe as a glowing orb of light, about the size of a passionfruit. I blinked, thinking I was imagining it, but it was still there, gently hovering. Then it slowly rose a little higher and vanished into thin air.

I was dumbfounded by what had just happened.

That night, I had a very vivid dream. I was performing an energy-healing ritual in a temple carved into a cave high in the mountains and healing someone lying on a huge stone slab. I woke up in the morning, wrote it down in my journal, and forgot about it.

A few months later, I had a conversation with my friend Kerry, who encouraged me to explore energy healing as part of my recovery from my spinal cord injury.

The very next day, I attended the One Heart Festival, a beautiful event in the heart of London's Ladbroke Grove, created to uplift and unite the local community in tribute to the neighbors we lost in the Grenfell Tower fire tragedy.

The first stall I saw, after arriving with my daughter, was a Pranic Healing stand. I was approached by a lady called Bella Clark, who radiated light from the inside out. She offered me a taster healing session and my spirit immediately responded with a full-body 'yes,' especially with yesterday's conversation with Kerry about energy healing fresh in my mind. It was undeniably synchronistic.

After feeling the powerful benefits of a short taster session, I later went on to work with Bella, an incredible Pranic therapist and mentor who supported me in working through my physical pain and trauma, and healing old limitations, including my fear of driving on the motorway. After many powerful sessions together, she encouraged me to train in Pranic Healing myself. The transformation I'd experienced made the decision very easy, so I jumped at the opportunity.

I couldn't believe my eyes on the first day of Level One training. Right there on the front cover of the course manual was an image of an orb of light that was identical to the one I'd seen floating above my altar.

Later in the session, I learned from Les Flitcroft, founder of the Institute of Pranic Healing UK and Ireland and a direct student of Master Choa Kok Sui, the modern-day founder of Pranic Healing, that the image was of an energetic presentation of a healing angel.

I had goosebumps all over my body and nearly launched out of my seat to interrupt the room to say, 'I saw one of those, I saw one of those!' It took every fiber of my being to stay focused on the lecture and not disrupt the whole training with my 'paranormal' experience.

At the first opportunity, when we broke for a toilet break, I pulled my journal out of my backpack on a mission to find the entry about my encounter with the orb. It was then that I remembered the dream that I'd had the same night about energy healing.

This is what a relationship with your guides can look like. It's not always linear or obvious, but the signs, the breadcrumbs, and the energy are all guiding you back to yourself, your healing, your power, and your purpose.

Soul-Inquiry Journal Prompts

Respond to these prompts by coming out of your head and dropping into your heart energy. Don't overthink your answers; just become aware of what comes up. Trust the subtle answers that arise.

~ What fears or beliefs do I still hold that make it difficult to fully trust my intuitive or spiritual connection?

~ Where did those stories originate? Is the idea still true for me now or is it outdated?

~ When did I receive guidance that I didn't recognize as guidance at the time?

~ What recurring patterns or synchronicities have I noticed lately? (If any - don't force them or make them fit.)

~ What might I hear from within or from my guides if I slowed down and truly listened?

Building a Relationship with Your Guides

Building a relationship with your guides isn't about becoming psychic or a medium *per se*, although you may feel called to develop to that level. It definitely isn't about becoming dependent on your guides, forcing 'signs' to fit, or using them as an excuse for inaction. It's about creating the conditions that make it easier to hear and recognize the golden breadcrumbs placed along your path. It's about feeling held, inspired, and guided as you navigate your life.

It's also about *integrating* what you receive: sitting with the wisdom, *embodying* the message, and, importantly, taking aligned action, but more about that later in the book. Here, we'll explore how you can create and strengthen the connection.

Creating a Supportive Connection

- **Tune in to energy signatures:** Don't get caught up too much in who your guides are or what their names are. If that unfolds naturally, great, but don't force it. Focus on how they feel. Some may feel maternal, others cosmic, nature-based, visual, and telepathic. They may be a group consciousness or a single entity. Do you feel a presence standing behind you? Or above you or in front of you? Does it feel like wisdom dropping in, a wash of cleansing and healing, or energetic upliftment? Just notice what you notice and let the relationship reveal itself over time.
- **Where/when to connect:** Guides aren't bound by time or space, so you don't need a special place to reach yours, but having a regular connection practice can deepen your relationship. You can set the intention to meet with your guides daily at your altar or invite them to walk with you as you move through life. Call on them before a road trip, a big meeting, a tough decision, as you walk home alone late at night, or if you're feeling stuck in heavy energies. The more consistently you connect, the more supportive and natural the relationship will become.
- **Keep a spirit journal:** As we know, spirit speaks in whispers and breadcrumbs. High-vibration energy moves quickly, and it can be surprisingly easy to forget details if we don't write them down. Record everything – dreams, signs, intuitive downloads, inner nudges, synchronicities, songs, and messages. You might not understand it all at first, but patterns often reveal themselves over time.

- **Give thanks:** Thank your guides for the signs, the nudges, the support. When a sign pops up, 'Thank you, guides,' when a download comes through, 'Thank you, guides,' when you invoke their presence, guidance, or protection, 'Thank you, guides.'

A Word on Cleansing, Boundaries, and Vibrational Integrity

If you're energetically sensitive, you may sometimes pick up lower-vibrational energy from people or places, or environmental psychic debris.

If you feel anything encroaching on your energy field that brings unease or heaviness, you can simply say:

'Only energies of the highest light, love,
and truth may enter this space.'

Ask unserving and low-vibe energies to be healed, transmuted, and returned to the light.

If the energy feels resistant, invite your high-vibe guides to help you clear the space. I like to call angelic energies into all corners of my home to maintain a high-vibrational space.

Mini-Checklist for Discerning Spirit Guidance

- *Does it feel loving, even if it stretches me?* True guidance might take you beyond your comfort zone, but it won't come with fear, shame, or force. It supports your growth, not your self-doubt.
- *Is it aligned with my highest good and the greater good?* Real guidance doesn't pander to ego or feed drama. It may not always

be what you want to hear, but it'll feel right. It'll bring you closer to integrity, truth, and what serves your soul and the collective.

- *Do I feel calm, clear, and grounded in my body when I receive it?* Even if the message surprises you, it often comes with a sense of expansiveness or sparks gentle curiosity. Your body might feel soft, centered, or lightly activated, but not tight, anxious, or overwhelmed.
- *Is it an invitation, not a demand?* Your guides won't pressure or manipulate you; their messages aren't wrapped in fear. If something feels pushy or panicked, take a breath, pause, tune in, and feel where it's coming from.
- *Have I created space to really listen?* It's hard to hear through the noise of emotion, overthinking, or distraction. Ground yourself. Breathe. Be present enough to notice what's beneath the surface. Do you need to do a busy brain download (*see p.34*) to clear some space to receive?
- *Has it been gently repeating or showing up through synchronicities?* Spirit tends to speak in patterns. A sign, symbol, phrase, or message that keeps reappearing is often your guides' way of flagging something important for your attention.

The Longing to Connect

Connection to your energy guides can be so delicious and intoxicating. When you connect to those otherworldly high-frequency energies of divine love, it's like tasting a nectar so sweet, hydrating, and nourishing to the palate that you want to drink every last available drop.

The vibe can be so high that you want to root in and live in that space, not just pitch up for a holiday before you return to the mundane.

It's easy to find yourself chasing the highs, but you often end up searching in that very act of seeking. And how can you connect to the golden frequencies of light if you're vibrating in lack and focused on what's missing? In my experience, spirit isn't summoned in desperation. It arrives in surrender, in the comfort of the present.

Chasing the highs can cause your guides to step back. They're not there for ego performance or emotional dependency; they're there to support your evolution. This is your human life; you're here to live and experience it and integrate wisdom, not to escape through constant spiritual seeking. If you find yourself in this energy of desperation, connect back to gratitude, to beauty, to that which lights you up, to being in the present, and rest in the holding of the subtle.

Our guides are with us through all of life, not just the high-vibe moments and manifestations of contact. Even in the moments when they may feel beyond reach, know that they're holding space for you energetically.

Your timing isn't their timing, and their timing isn't your timing, so just trust in divine timing. Everything unfolds when it's intended to. Let go of any temptation to control outcomes.

Sometimes your guides will hand you a golden thread, a vision, a word, a concept, an inner knowing. Still, if you're always looking up, waiting for the next thread, without ever anchoring the last one, you'll miss the opportunity to root and grow what you've already been given.

Guidance isn't just about receiving, it's about embodying. It's about anchoring it into your vibration through intentional and aligned action.

Think of it this way: Your guides might offer you a seed of potential, but you're the one who has to plant it, nurture it, water it with your actions, tend to it with patience, give it space to grow, and let natural energies do their thing.

Find your rhythm.

Receive graciously.

Ground. Integrate. Embody.

LIGHT ACTIVATION

Invoking Your Guides

If you're ready to establish and deepen your connection to your high-vibe energy guides, let's begin invoking them now.

- Create a quiet space for yourself.
- Light a white candle, holding the intention to signal to your guides, your soul, and the universe that you're ready to connect.
- Now energetically ground yourself down through the soles of your feet, visualizing roots anchoring you deep in the earth.
- Visualize or imagine receiving light and high-vibrational energy through the crown of your head, allowing them to illuminate your body as they flow down into your roots and into the earth.
- With a deep breath, pull the energy back through into your heart space.

- When you feel ready, whether it's out loud or quietly within, say the following or be guided to write your own resonant invocation, but be specific about invoking high-vibrational guides:

> *'I call upon my high-vibrational energy guides. In the name of my greatest good and the greater good of all, I invite your healing, wisdom, guidance, love, and protection. I am open and ready to receive. With gratitude, so be it, so be it, and so it is.'*

- As your energetic intention reverberates across time and space, trust that your call has been received.
- Now, for a moment, just sit quietly in the energy of the invocation and be present with the energy of possibility.
- Let whatever's meant to come... come. Maybe it's a sensation, a word, a subtle shift in the atmosphere around you. Maybe it's just peace or a sense of potential.
- Breathe.
- Let the energy move through you.
- Let it settle.
- If you feel called to do so, journal any reflections.

. . . .

CHAPTER 10

Your Body of Light

'When you bring healing to your energy body, in addition to the layers of your heart and mind, you lay the foundation for a transformation that changes you at your very essence.'

At its core, your body of light is the subtle energy system that powers your multidimensional experience, intermingling with your physical body and the infinite energies of existence.

Life flows well when your energy body and your physical body are in harmony. When they're aligned, you feel vibrant, grounded, connected, and more in integrity with your soul essence. But when your energy body is blocked, stagnant, or depleted, you can experience anxiety, burnout, fatigue, emotional overwhelm, physical issues, or a loitering funk.

I'm meeting a lot of people at the moment who are run down and persistently ill with colds and minor ailments, and so often they aren't observing the bigger energetic picture.

The clearer your energy body, the brighter your light, and the more effectively your mind, body, and soul can function.

In the last chapter, we explored our clair senses, and it's important to know that energetic debris in the chakras and auric field can cloud our ability to receive wisdom from our guides clearly. In fact, it can impact our ability to receive on all levels.

Awareness of Your Energy Body

A key part of raising your vibration and supporting your life-force energy is developing an awareness of your energy body. With this conscious awareness, you can intuitively work with your light body to facilitate healing and receive wisdom.

This is the real secret sauce, the key to lasting healing and manifesting your best life in a way that's authentic, aligned, and energetically in integrity with your potential. So there's no time like the present to bring the energy body into the conversation.

Our natural state of being is to be in harmony, and our soul potential and the vital energy of the universe want to flow through us. But through the abrasiveness of the human experience, we often forget this. When we regain our awareness, we can be proactive about keeping our energetic channels open, clear, and free from accumulating debris.

Imagine yourself as a wind instrument, like panpipes – energy in and energy out. When you're in alignment, that energy flows through you with ease, playing a beautiful tune. When you're out of alignment and riddled with stagnant energy, it causes congestion on your energetic superhighway, impacting the quality of the tune you play.

Just as you did with the energy in your home, it's time to move through your energetic body, clearing out what no longer belongs to you, so that you can bring in more energy and light to support the evolved version of yourself that you're becoming.

This part of the work leaves no stone unturned, and the body of light is a deep subject. It houses many layers of truth and evolving wisdom. Just as you begin to think you understand it, more layers reveal themselves. So, don't overwhelm yourself. At this stage, you just need to know enough to support the next phase of your healing. After that, if your intuition is guiding you deeper, allow yourself to follow your curiosity.

The quality of your inner world radiates through your energy, there's no hiding it.

Your thoughts, words, actions, and intentions sit in your field, contributing to the frequency you carry and the vibes you're putting out.

Have you ever met someone who smiles and wishes you well, but your sensory perception picks up that their energy isn't in integrity with what they're portraying? Energetically sensitive people can perceive that dissonance between a person's true energy and intention and the image they're trying to project.

A clairvoyant would be able to observe the status of someone's chakra system in a way that painted a very vivid and accurate picture of their experience. A person with strong clairsentient perception might feel into someone's energy body to sense where energetic issues might lie.

This is where you find yourself standing truly naked in the illumination of your energetics.

That's why integrity matters, not just in what you say, but also in what you do, who you are, and what you're willing to confront. Your energetic evolution calls for radical self-responsibility.

In that expansion of your conscious awareness, your healing is given the opportunity to root in even more deeply, not just in your mind or emotions, but in every layer of your physical and non-physical being.

When you activate your body of light by bringing healing and cleansing to your energetic 'wounds,' you improve the quality of your human experience and become a more rounded and compassionate person, a more effective channel for divine wisdom, and a highly effective manifester of your soul's desires.

This is where you start remembering who you really came here to be.

The Components of Your Light Body

Your light body is made up of your aura (your energetic field), your chakras (energy centers), and subtle channels called meridians or *nadis*, and they help life-force energy, also known as *prana*, *chi*, *mana*, or the spirit of life, to flow through you. Life-force energy is like the breath of life that moves through all living things.

Your aura is the field of energy that surrounds your body, like an invisible glow that reflects your thoughts, emotions, and vitality. It's both protective and expressive in the way that holds the imprint of your inner world while also radiating your energy outward.

The meridians and nadis are the subtle channels within you, like little rivers of light that carry life-force energy through our physical and non-physical body.

When these channels are clear, energy can flow freely, and you'll feel balanced and full of vitality, but when they become blocked you might notice tension, fatigue, or emotional heaviness.

Along with our chakras, these elements form our body of light.

Understanding the chakra system will bring you an even closer relationship with your body of light.

Chakras have become a bit of a buzzword among spiritual seekers and influencers across social media, but this system is more than just a trend for us to pick up and play with for our pleasure.

Although it's often simplified in modern wellness spaces, the chakra system is deeply nuanced. It's a deep and complex subject. It's an ancient spiritual framework originating from India, rooted in early yogic, Vedic, and Tantric traditions. These teachings, which date back thousands of years, were originally passed down through sacred oral and written lineages in Sanskrit. *Chakra* is a Sanskrit word meaning 'wheel.' The energy centers of the subtle body are described as spinning wheels or vortexes.

I'm not a Sanskrit scholar. What I share is drawn from my personal experience and understanding, shaped through spiritual and psychic development classes, textbooks, and my training in energy healing. While these perspectives have been deeply pivotal in my own healing journey, they represent a modern, adapted lens of a system with much deeper roots.

I encourage anyone exploring this path to go beyond a surface-level understanding. Learn about the original texts from which this wisdom stems and seek to understand the cultures from which it was birthed. Seek out the voices and teachers who carry these lineages forward with integrity.

Let's all continue to deepen our understanding, honor the cultures that birthed the teachings, and carry them with the integrity and respect that they deserve.

What follows is just a glance into the shop window and an invitation to begin exploring how these energy centers may be showing up in your own life.

For the sake of this book, we'll look at the seven major chakras that run from the base of our spine to the top of our head, like power points that help energy flow through us.

When our chakras are aligned or in balance, they support our vitality and the smooth flow of life-force energy through us.

If they're blocked, it can be difficult for the energy to move, making us feel stuck on a ladder that we're unable to climb, limiting our progress in life.

Each chakra is connected to a different part of our body and different aspects of our life.

Root Chakra

Location: Base of the spine

Color: Red

Represents: Basic survival, safety, security, belonging, trust in life

Unhealthy presentation: Chronic fear or anxiety, hoarding, feeling disconnected from the body, hypervigilance, beliefs around scarcity or unworthiness, emotional sensitivity, rigidity, aggression, disorganization, ancestral and family connection issues, lower back pain, leg, feet or hip issues, fatigue

Healthy presentation: Feeling grounded, safe, and supported, trust in the process of life, a strong connection to your body and the present moment, steady finances and a secure home life, inner calm and resilience

How to heal: Grounding, time in nature, aromatherapy, cultivating certainty and safety, gardening, yoga, eating nourishing root vegetables like potato, yam, carrot, and dasheen, ginger tea

Root Chakra Connection Journal Prompts

- When did I first feel that the world wasn't a safe place for me?
- Where in my life do I feel unsafe, unsupported, or unstable, physically, emotionally, or financially?
- Is my body communicating my relationship with survival through pain, tension, or fatigue?

Sacral Chakra

Location: Lower abdomen, just below the navel

Color: Orange

Represents: Emotions, creativity, sensuality, sexuality, pleasure, relationships

Unhealthy presentation: Reproductive or menstrual issues, womb trauma, sexual shame or disconnection from sensuality, creative blocks or a lack of inspiration, intimacy issues, difficulty expressing emotions, codependent relationship patterns, low self-worth, guilt around desires, a lost sense of fun, control issues, menstrual imbalances, sexual dysfunction

Healthy presentation: Emotional flow and authenticity, creative vitality and expression, healthy intimacy and sexual energy, a deep sense of pleasure, joy, and self-worth, emotional sensitivity and emotional intuition, a feeling of being in the flow, spontaneity

How to heal: Play, joy, intuitive dance and movement, painting, bathing and oil rituals, a womb ceremony, orange juice

Sacral Chakra Connection Journal Prompts

~ How has shame or guilt shaped the way I experience intimacy, creativity, or self-worth?

~ Where am I suppressing my creativity or sensuality?

~ Whose stories or beliefs about sensuality or creativity am I still carrying?

Solar Plexus Chakra

Location: Upper abdomen, above the navel and below the ribs

Color: Yellow

Represents: Personal power, self-esteem, confidence, willpower, identity

Unhealthy presentation: Low self-confidence or self-doubt, anger, frustration, or control issues, overthinking, people-pleasing, inactivity or procrastination, digestive problems, fatigue, difficulty setting boundaries, powerlessness, fear of failure, stomach cramps or nausea, blood-sugar imbalances

Healthy presentation: Motivation, confidence, and a strong will, a clear sense of identity and purpose, healthy boundaries and assertiveness, the ability to take inspired action and make decisions, empowered self-expression and inner strength, focus

How to heal: Breathwork, candle gazing to embody the energy of fire, core strengthening practices, empowerment rituals

Solar Plexus Chakra Connection Journal Prompts

- How does my body respond when I feel powerless or out of control?
- What would it look like to fully own my energy and take up space?
- What am I really afraid would happen if I fully owned my power?

Heart Chakra

Location: Center of the chest

Color: Green

Represents: Love, compassion, forgiveness, emotional healing, connection, a bridge between the lower and upper chakras, physical and spiritual integration

Unhealthy presentation: Emotional withdrawal or bitterness, over-giving or over-attachment in relationships, fear of vulnerability or rejection, holding on to past heartbreak or resentment, loneliness, grief, or mistrust, difficulty receiving or giving love, disconnection, repulsion to touch, a tight chest or shortness of breath, heart palpitations, lung issues

Healthy presentation: Compassionate, open-hearted relationships, deep empathy and emotional presence, healthy balance of giving and receiving, self-love and inner peace, a sense of oneness with others and life

How to heal: Forgiveness practices, heart-to-heart hugs, connecting with animals, heart-expanding playlists, acts of kindness

Heart Chakra Connection Journal Prompts

~ Am I still holding grief, heartbreak, or resentment in my heart?

~ How might past pain show up through the way I relate to myself or others today?

~ Am I ready to love myself in the way I've always longed to be loved?

Throat Chakra

Location: Throat and neck area

Color: Blue

Represents: Communication, self-expression, truth, authenticity

Unhealthy presentation: Fear of speaking up or being misunderstood, not advocating for yourself or hiding your truth, an inhibited voice, not living your authentic purpose, silence in the face of injustice, fear of being seen or heard, public-speaking fear, recurring sore throats or tonsillitis, thyroid imbalances, neck and jaw tension, voice issues

Healthy presentation: Honest, clear, and authentic expression, the ability to listen deeply and communicate effectively, speaking your truth with compassion, expressing creativity and ideas with ease, a strong sense of alignment between thoughts and speech

How to heal: Sound and vibrational healing, singing, speaking your truth, starting a YouTube channel or podcast, communicating your authenticity

Throat Chakra Connection Journal Prompts

~ Where in my life am I not honoring my voice or my boundaries?

~ What am I afraid might happen if I express myself fully?

~ Am I over-explaining myself to be understood?

Third Eye Chakra

Location: Between the eyebrows

Color: Indigo

Represents: Intuition, inner vision, perception, insight, consciousness

Unhealthy presentation: Mental fog, confusion, or lack of direction, disconnection from inner guidance or gut feelings, overreliance on logic or skepticism, dismissiveness of dreams or intuition, closed-mindedness or rigid beliefs, escapism, no imagination, issues with visualization, no dream recall, no bigger-picture perspective, tension headaches or migraines, sleep disturbances or nightmares, sinus issues, eye strain or tension between the brows

Healthy presentation: Strong intuition and inner knowing, imagination, clear insight and mental clarity, vivid dreams and visionary thinking, connection to deeper meaning and a spiritual perspective, the ability to see through illusions

How to heal: Visualization practices, creating a vision board, using oracle cards or divination tools

Third Eye Chakra Connection Journal Prompts

- Where am I ignoring my intuition?
- What am I afraid I'll see if I fully open to my intuitive vision?
- Am I really ready to live in alignment with my inner vision, even if it defies logic or comfort?

Crown Chakra

Location: Crown of the head

Colors: Violet/White

Represents: Higher consciousness, divine connection, enlightenment, purpose

Unhealthy presentation: Feeling spiritually lost or disconnected, depression, skepticism, over-intellectualizing spirituality without embodiment, resistance to guidance or universal truths, feeling unsupported by the universe, spiritual bypassing, spiritual emptiness, dizziness, brain-related issues, sensitivity to light or sound

Healthy presentation: A sense of purpose, clarity, and spiritual connection, feeling guided and aligned with universal wisdom, inner peace, and expanded awareness, connection to something greater than the self, openness to divine inspiration

How to heal: Meditation, prayer, surrender practices, presence at your altar, energy healing

Crown Chakra Journal Connection Prompts

- Is my physical exhaustion or mental overwhelm linked to a deeper need for spiritual (re)connection?
- Am I allowing space for stillness and for divine insight to land in my life?
- What am I afraid might happen if I fully trust my spiritual path?

Did any of those chakra presentations speak to you? Did any of the messages about health, or where you may be feeling stuck, resonate with you?

The following Light Activation will guide you into deeper communion with your energy body, helping you observe and hold space for healing that may be ready to rise.

Allow your chakras to speak. You don't have to figure anything out, just be present, be curious, and trust what emerges.

As we bring this chapter and the activation stage of your journey to a close, take a moment to honor how far you've come. You've opened the door to deep energetic awareness, cleared old imprints, and reconnected with the subtle intelligence of your soul. Through this healing work, you've not only tended to your past, but also tuned your energy field so that you can receive more light, more clarity, more wisdom, and more life.

Onward we move.

LIGHT ACTIVATION

Seven-Day Chakra Connection

This activation helps you reconnect with your seven key chakras, tune in to their wisdom, and release what no longer serves you, so you can raise your vibration and your light to the next level.

Meet your energetic self without pressure, expectation, or judgment, just awareness. Don't second-guess yourself, just trust yourself, trust the whispers, and notice any memories, thoughts, or feelings that crop up.

- To embody the energy, healing, and revitalization of the chakra of the day, you can dress in its corresponding color and consume similarly colored fruits, vegetables, and natural juices.
    - Root: Red
    - Sacral: Orange
    - Solar Plexus: Yellow
    - Heart: Green
    - Throat: Blue
    - Third Eye: Indigo
    - Crown: Violet/White
- To begin this reconnection, drop into your presence.
- Invoke the guidance, protection, and wisdom of your guides.
- Center yourself with a breath.
- Imagine those roots running down through the base of your spine, down your legs, and into the earth, anchoring you, and helping you feel held and supported.
- Focus your awareness on your energy body and its subtle wisdom.
- Set the intention to release any stagnant and outdated energies to allow the light of your soul's truth to flow through your energy system unhindered by what no longer serves you.
- Starting at the base of your spine and moving upward, tap into the energy of each chakra, using the power of your intention and your breath. Use your strongest clair sense to help you visualize, feel, hear, etc., a swirling wheel of light in each chakra's associated color (*see above*).

- Ask: 'What do you need me to know?' and 'Do you need to receive energy or release energy?'

....

Now, before we step into the final stage of this book, I invite you to join me in the following channeled activation (*opposite*) to release, renew, and emerge, ready to expand.

LIGHTWORK

Release, Renew, Emerge

*'Release the grip of your trauma, fear,
and sadness. Let go of the residue of the past.
Call in renewal and revitalization,
and rise to meet the light of your soul.'*

You've done so beautifully to arrive here, to have allowed your curiosity to keep you reading, perhaps even despite some discomfort at times, moving through the pages and deepening your connection to your authentic soul self.

So far, you've peeled back the layers of conditioning, revealed buried patterns, opened up to your energetic soul self, and courageously held space for your healing.

You've remembered more of who you really are, and now you're poised on the threshold of meeting your highest possibilities.

Before you step into the final phase of this book, this is your opportunity to release the last strands of outdated stories, beliefs, and burdens that have limited your potential.

We're creating space for your fullest expression to emerge.

This activation is a channeled visualization that supports reconnecting with your inner light. It invites you to meet the luminous essence of your highest self, sever the energetic ties that have weighed you down, and bathe in the healing waters of renewal.

You can receive the energy by listening to the activation (either recording yourself reading it aloud or else downloading the audio book from the usual places) or participating on a deeper level by setting a sacred space, closing your eyes, and journeying with me.

So, if you wish to, find your quiet space. Let your breath soften and your shoulders relax.

Trust in your readiness for the next stage of your evolution, and let's begin. It's time to come home to the highest, most brilliant version of yourself.

1. Release

- Take a deep breath, connect with your belly, and exhale through your mouth.
- Just resting behind the soft blackness of your closed eyes, you feel yourself being drawn forward, positively magnetized by an energy beckoning you forward. It feels comforting and familiar.
- In your mind's eye, you feel called to gently flutter open your eyes. You notice a spot of light on the floor ahead of you, step into its inviting glow, and bathe for a moment in its warmth.
- You see a bright light out in the distance. You notice a familiar figure silhouetted by it and you feel deep peace and ease in its presence.
- You notice a golden thread on the floor in front of you. You feel called to pick it up and follow it. It connects you to the figure in the light up ahead.

- You start to walk confidently toward the light. Its familiarity increases your confidence as you walk toward it, step by step, with increasing purpose.
- The silhouette in the golden light becomes clearer. It's you, the highest, most expansive version of you, a glistening, glimmering, crystalline version of you, your ancient soul essence. It represents your highest possible energy.
- For this exercise, we'll visualize this whole soul self as a golden energy body, sparkling, translucent, luminous, and magnificent.
- Your soul self holds out their glistening hand, and you take it. You notice a warm glow in your heart space; as you inhale, the glow extends outward.
- Your soul self encapsulates your expansive essence; you're the human representative helping your soul to experience life here on Earth. They've never lost sight of you, but now, as you awaken and remember who you really are, you expand into more of who you're capable of becoming.
- You feel so deeply at ease as your soul starts to show you around, pointing outward into the vast and expansive space around you that's laced with golden threads of possibilities.
- Your soul points down at your feet, bringing into focus vines wrapped around your ankles. They've been gathering and holding you in their grip, slowly accumulating as you've traveled the path of life from birth to now. Now that they've been pointed out, you become aware of the sensation of their restriction.
- Your soul self hands you a pair of golden scissors and looks at you with an affirming soft nod, as if to gently encourage you to release what no longer serves you.

- As you prepare to cut the vines, thank them for having traveled with you all this way and let them know they're not needed where you're heading now.
- It's safe now to cut away the vines from the past.

2. Renew

- You become aware that you're deep in lush tropical rainforest, standing on rich, fertile soil - soil enriched by the falling of the dead leaves that have been surrendered by the tall trees that surround you.
- There are healing green hues in abundance around you.
- No one else is here, just the two of you. You're guided to a waterfall. The water tumbles into the stunning emerald pool below it.
- Take a breath, receive the beauty around you.
- Your soul invites you into the pool to cleanse yourself. You take off your clothing, noticing how it feels to be standing bare, held in Mother Nature's arms.
- You step forward toward the emerald pool to test the temperature of the water.
- As you dip your toes in, the water feels warm and irresistibly inviting.
- Cool droplets of spray from the falling water refresh your senses as they kiss your face.
- You wade into the pool up to your waist, make your way over to the waterfall, and ease yourself back under its flow, tipping your head back into the water to cleanse your crown before bringing your whole body underneath its cleansing flow, feeling the upliftment as the healing waters wash away the dust and debris of outdated patterns of the past.

- The water cleanses every particle of you and your energetic field.
- You pause here, under the water, acknowledging what it feels like to feel lighter, unburdened by past weight.

3. Emerge

- When the moment feels right, you emerge, noticing a greater capacity to take a deep breath.
- Breathe into that.
- As you take a moment to breathe, your body dries off in the warm sun.
- Your soul hands you a golden hooded cloak. You take it, wrap it around yourself, pull up your hood, and feel an energetic activation that upgrades you to a higher state of vibration. The cloak feels good on you. It makes you feel powerful, enriched, and ready for the journey ahead.
- Breathe into it. Have a moment of recognition as you honor where you've been and what you've overcome.
- Taking a final glance behind you before you move along on your journey, you notice your old clothes on the bank. They look tired and weathered. As you look at them, you see them turning to dust, then the dust pile settling into the earth.
- Defying the process of time, a most beautiful flower sprouts up in their place. I wonder what color it is?
- You approach the flower to smell its sweet perfume. Draw in its scent in a long and slow inhale through your nose, and exhale with an audible sigh. Notice how the fragrance makes you feel. Take a moment to admire its beauty before turning to follow your guide along the pathway forward.

- Soul waits for you up ahead. The path through the healing rainforest looks like it's ending. It concludes at a viewing platform that looks out over your empowered future.
- Soul places an energetic safety harness around you.
- You look down at the next part of the journey. It's lush down there, deeply abundant and inviting. You feel excited about the next destination, but perhaps a little hesitant to take the leap.
- You tug gently at the straps of your harness, which feels reassuring. Soul puts their hand out. You take it. As you both leap, you feel supported by a parachute of surrounding energies.
- Below lies a huge cushioned throne, perfectly placed for your gentle landing. Soul looks at you and says, 'You've got this now,' before gently releasing your hand just as you're about to reach the comfort of your soft, pillowy throne.
- Soul lets you know that you can call on them at any time by slowing down, connecting to your breath, and dropping your focus into your heart space, for this is where they can be found, in the seat of your heart-centered awareness.
- As you sit comfortably on your throne, take a deep breath to anchor into the journey and another deep breath to connect to the present moment and your seat.
- If your eyes are closed, slowly wiggle your fingers and toes or just bring your awareness back to your body.
- Roll your neck gently if it's comfortable for you to do so and open your eyes when you're ready.
- Say, 'And so it is.'

PART III

Expand

Open · Expand · Illuminate

Step into the light of
who you came here to be.

CHAPTER 11

Your Illuminated Future

'Your journey to embodying your illuminated self begins the moment you dare to conjure them in your mind's eye. Envision them, dream big, and allow this highest version of yourself to expand into spaces beyond what you can yet imagine... and then, bring them to life with intentional action.'

I hope you're feeling lighter as you're moving through this book and that you can sense yourself expanding page by page. This is where the fun really begins as we set about creating a vision for your illuminated future. And when I say 'illuminated future,' I mean a future that's empowered by the light that you're activating within and the relationship that you're nurturing with our energetic universe.

Now's a great time to shed light on your future self and activate its potential.

Your empowered future self is but a few energetic and behavioral shifts away. To make those adjustments, you first need to connect with the vision that's waiting to emerge. This chapter is where you look for clues to your potential in your existing passions and set about taking aligned action to harmonize with the powerful frequency of who you're becoming. It closes with a Light Activation that connects you to an energetic vision of your life five years from now.

This is one of my favorite parts of the journey. It's where you begin the process of connecting to the true creator magic that you really came here to embody, as an extension of the creative energy that sparked your existence.

You reclaim your power by reconnecting with the ability to create your own experience. You do this by taking control of your thoughts, being intentional about your actions, and shaping the things you want to see and be in the world.

In the timeline of our history, a system of hierarchy was established. Through that process, those at the top of their respective societal hierarchies dictated their creative vision to the rest, forcing everyone else to conform, often with just a few renegades on the fringes who challenged the status quo. These individuals were often outcast, demonized, belittled, or disregarded as being mentally unsound, before their dissenting voices had the chance to spark widespread revolt.

Over time, we became servants of the vision of the privileged few, losing our sense of power along the way as we all mindlessly followed the societal standards set before us.

Look out at the world, my friend. I don't know about you, but I think there's much room for improvement. It's high time that we all looked at the world and questioned how we ended up here.

Instead of mindlessly following the will of others and the socially accepted standards, it's time to dare to dream, and dream big.

Your Soul's Desire

Take a moment to sink into your heart, connect deeply within, and see what your soul wants you to create, from a grounded place, a conscious place, from a place of healing and self-awareness, and for the greater good of yourself, your family, your community, and wider humanity.

- Can you imagine a life where you're healing, in your power, and creating your vision, on your terms?
- Feel into that, allow that energetic resonance to reverberate through your being.
- Imagine a life where you wake up every day energized by your purpose and excited about the life you're creating.

The more people who work with this intention, the more it helps us create a world where people live from their heart, are connected to their soul, and pour light back into humanity instead of projecting from pain and disconnection.

The best part is that you get to have fun as you experiment, expand, and step into your creative power, while doing your bit to build a better world. What better legacy could there be?

The Power of Clarity

At this stage of the process, you might feel energized by the healing work you've done so far and excited about the possibilities ahead, yet still unsure about how your path will unfold. This is a very natural part of the process. Gaining clarity is often a journey in itself.

When you sense that you're made for more but aren't sure where to begin, it can feel extremely frustrating. Like standing at the entry point of a maze, knowing there's a destination inside, but being faced with tall hedges that obscure your view, and twists and turns on an unknown pathway.

The Light Activation at the end of this chapter will help you nurture a bigger-picture vision that grows clearer over time.

The clues to your illuminated future can often be found in the things that light you up and activate an energy of excitement within you. The energetic resonance that says 'yes,' and the vibes that say 'no' are equally powerful navigational tools.

When you begin to get clear on who you really are, what lights you up, and what you're creating, whether it's for your life in general, your relationships, healing, soul growth, or business goals, life shifts. You're no longer stuck in the stifling quagmire of a fuzzy lack of vision or frustration.

When you start to get clear, so does the universe – and so the opportunities, the boundaries, the decisions, the relationships, and the spirit nudges all become clear, too.

When you create clarity, you transform the ways you spend your days. You move with purpose and confidence. You know what's for you and what to let pass you by.

You become so finely attuned to your vibration and that of others that your decision-making process becomes impeccable. It doesn't mean you no longer meet resistance and setbacks, but they now become powerful tools for your navigation, with your illuminated self acting like a lighthouse to keep you on track.

Your growing trust in the process helps you to feel deeply rooted and composed, even in the face of the inevitable stormy waters of life. Your root chakra is regulating and strengthening through this healing process. The way you face life is changing. You're shifting out of survival mode, and when you feel rooted, you've more capacity for your energy to rise. As you begin to trust, your energy moves up from a previously dysregulated root chakra, bringing light to matters of the sacral chakra, where you can more easily allow yourself to explore your creativity and birth new possibilities.

Is Your Creativity Being Fully Embodied?

Do you have a list of things in your notes app that you might like to create 'one day'? Do you have an inescapable feeling that you aren't yet fulfilling your potential?

One of my greatest frustrations in life was feeling I had a greater purpose, but not having a clue what it was. Looking back now, I can join the dots of things that lit me up and how they now play a key role in my life. But back in school, I had no idea what I wanted to be in life. I struggled with an education system that made me feel like I was supposed to have it all figured out by the time I was doing my end-of-school exams, but who *really* knows themselves at 15?

In my younger years, I bounced purposelessly from job to job, from McDonald's to waitressing, to cooking greasy English breakfasts in cafés, to pub kitchens. I was a sports-store assistant, a charity street collector, an agency worker, and a record-shop assistant, before settling down to a soulless but socially acceptable 'career' in banking.

While I didn't know what I wanted to do professionally, one passion that remained constant throughout all those random jobs, and still does to this day, is my love of Jungle Drum and Bass music. It spoke to my soul in so many ways – the diversity and representation, the community, the creativity, and the sense of belonging that offered a connection that I never felt with mainstream culture.

I credit Jungle D&B for helping to save me after G's death. I'd get lost in the music, forget the weight of my grief and the monotony of daily life, and let my trauma get lost in the vibration of the bass, for a few hours at least.

It was through my love of D&B that I met Kane, who is a DJ and producer. It was also where I connected with some of my very best friends and greatest influences. The music radiated like a central sun that attracted like-minded, resonant souls. Like moths to a flame, we were pulled toward the underground subculture that generated its own light and built its own momentum.

Jungle D&B carved its own path away from the mainstream, fueled by unapologetic creative expression and a refusal to conform to mainstream norms. The scene emerged organically when people dared to experiment and follow what excited them. In expressing their truth and their own unique light, they created a sound in which the under-represented, the rebellious, and the underdog could unite.

The Jungle D&B scene thrived by refusing to dim itself to fit in. It became a living example of the magnetic power of being unapologetically yourself.

I wonder what passions you have in your life, and what they might represent to you?

My obsession with the genre began in the 90s. One of the first tunes to truly mesmerize me was a track called 'Warhead' by an artist named Krust, which came out in 1997, when I was 14.

Krust, aka K, is a true pioneer, constantly pushing boundaries and at the forefront of genre-defining production. He was a member of the Mercury Music Award-winning collective Reprazent and co-owner of the Full Cycle record label. Beyond his pioneering status in the music industry, today he's also the co-founder of one of Europe's first CBD companies, Amma Life, as well as a creative consultant. He's a respected voice and a man of great lived experience and wisdom.

From listening to his music back in the day, I credit him *today* with being a key mentor who helped me reach the next level in my life. The Light Activation at the end of this chapter is inspired by one of his powerful expansive practices.

Seeking Answers

In the immediate months after my spinal cord injury, I had the inescapable sense that there were deep lessons I needed to learn about what had happened to me, and I was searching for answers. I set about absorbing every bit of knowledge I could get my hands on. From books to podcasts to audiobooks, I was on a mission to answer the call to self-examine.

Kane sent me an episode of K's podcast. It drew from his deep well of creative experience, business insight, and work as an NLP practitioner and coach. The way he spoke about mindset had an awakening impact on me, and before I knew it, I was on a call with him and joining his weekly mentoring group.

I'll never forget the first session I attended. K took us on a guided meditation to meet our future self. In this visualization exercise, the first seeds of my potential began to make themselves visible. I went deep into meditation and began to receive impressions about a book and the prospect of becoming an author.

It wasn't anything that I'd ever considered. I didn't know any authors, and growing up, the representation was so lacking that it wasn't even on my radar. I just figured that writing books was reserved for the White middle and upper classes. Not me, a working-class mixed-race kid from Birmingham. 'I don't see it, so I can't be it' was what my subconscious absorbed.

So, when the vision started to erupt, I didn't take it seriously at first. I noted it down in my journal after the session, but that was it. Each time I did the 'future self' visualization, the sense of the book would come back, but it was so far off my radar that my mind didn't compute the seeds that were being shown. At the time, I gathered that I was drawn to books as I was spending a lot of time reading children's books to my daughter, but my low expectations dismissed what was really coming through.

In June of 2020, the horrific murder of George Floyd sent shockwaves through the world. With large parts of the global population in lockdown and our collective attention fixed on the news and social media, the world was watching. George's murder heightened conversations around race, Black lives, and representation.

Throughout the years of my healing and soul growth, I deeply felt the absence of literature by people who looked like me and people with similar backgrounds, financial circumstances, and life experiences. I was reading books written by 'privileged,' well-connected authors who centered high-cost healing modalities and tropical retreats as the path to healing. It became hard to truly believe that deep healing and lasting prosperity were meant for everyday people, if this was apparently what it took to find peace.

Deep down, it never felt right to me. I knew people who looked like me, who carried immense wisdom, who had mastered the art of humble, joyful, present-moment living, and who were deeply connected to nature. They found contentment in a material-driven world that didn't center, or even fully see, their experience. So why weren't more of their stories on the bookshelves? The stories of those who didn't run away to 'find themselves.' The ones who never had the privilege of escaping. The ones who were forced to sit in their lot and mine it for answers. The ones who could teach what accessible healing truly looks like, for all.

I felt a deep sense of frustration. We're here. We buy the books, and we contribute significantly to the economy. So why are we still so under-represented in this genre? It's as if we're only allowed to speak on trauma and struggle, but what about the glow-up? What about the joy, the abundance, the success story on the other side of the pain?

When we aren't visible,
it's limiting what future generations
can believe is possible for them.

When we aren't visible, we limit the size of the dreams of others. But those are some of the consequences of those hierarchical societal structures that we spoke about earlier.

At the time that these frustrations were weighing extra heavy on my heart and mind, I was reading Dr Joe Dispenza's *You Are the Placebo*, sent to me by my friend Danny to support my healing journey. I recall turning my Joe Dispenza book sideways to see the publisher and heading straight to the Hay House website to see just how representative it was.

As I explored the site, I came across their Diverse Wisdom program, which was established to attract and promote more writers of color in the personal development, holistic health, and spirituality space. At that time, I'd no desire or ambition to be an author, mind you, but I felt encouraged by the fact that they had this initiative and that it had begun before the black square solidarity posts on Instagram and the knee-jerk DEI efforts of 2020.

With the work I'd been doing with K to rebuild my confidence, I decided to take representation into my own hands and launched the Curl Power podcast (later rebranded as Her Power). My aim was to share my own lessons from healing and personal development, as well as to interview other women making waves in representation, like Jamelia Donaldson, founder of Treasure Tress, the UK and Europe's first and largest product discovery box for textured hair, and Charlotte Stavrou (*née* Williams), founder of the inclusive influencer marketing agency SevenSix.

I hoped these conversations would inspire others like me, who needed to hear from people like them.

The podcast connected me with women from all over the world, women who messaged to say they felt seen through my words, that they could relate to my experiences, and that my techniques had helped them to overcome their challenges. Some even told me I should write a book. It was such a powerful confirmation that our voices do matter, that stories like ours deserve to be heard.

I felt more encouraged than ever to keep sharing, keep connecting, keep showing up. And it was around then that I really started to understand just how much of what I'd learned through navigating the hardest seasons of my life could actually support others, too.

About a year after launching the podcast, one July evening as I lay in bed on the cusp of sleep, Spirit popped in clairaudiently, repeating, 'Hay House published author, Hay House published author, Hay House published author,' until I had to say out loud, 'Okay, thank you, Spirit, I hear you.'

That's random, I thought, before falling off to sleep.

The next morning, I woke up, checked my inbox, and there was an email from the Hay House marketing team advertising their upcoming writers' workshop. It sounded exciting, but I knew I wouldn't be able to attend because I'd lost my income after my injury. However, my curiosity prompted me to click and read more, and at the bottom, I saw a mention of the Diverse Wisdom initiative and Lousie Hay's bursary scheme. It was the program I'd seen on the website a couple of years previously. My entire spirit responded with an electric excitement.

I couldn't believe it. Just the night before, when Spirit had been saying, 'Hay House published author,' had they actually been talking about me?

I had to apply. Even if I didn't know exactly what I was doing, everything in me said this was aligned. All the signs were pointing to it. So I followed my guidance, wrote my 500-word application, and applied on the spot.

Now I felt ready to answer a call that I would once never even have considered. I was actually starting not only to dream big, but also to take action toward the big vision that was emerging.

Beginning Your Expansion

This is *your* invitation to dream big. Open up to possibilities that are so wild that they won't even register on the frame of your experience for now. Soul is calling you to expand into places that you've never been. So don't disregard the seeds that emerge as being unattainable. I mean, here I am, after all that, a Hay House-published author, and here you are, reading my book.

Remain open to all possibilities, because it's very possible that your illuminated life might far surpass what you currently believe to be possible.

Everything around you began with a simple thought that evolved into action and became manifest.

Create the Conditions

To truly allow your soul self to step up and lead, you need to create the conditions for the whispers of your higher self to be seen, felt, or heard.

Make creative, intentional space for the seeds of your future to land. Invite your soul to bring forward insights about who you really came here to be. Just like K did for me, give your creative imagination permission to explore new possibilities and nurture them into becoming.

It's time to connect with a greater vision. Zoom out and see the potential timelines waiting in the ether for you to bring your human self and soul self into alignment. Think beyond tomorrow and start imagining where you want to be five years from now. Create space for your soul's potential to download.

Self-Inquiry Journal Prompts

Explore your wildest dreams. Ask yourself:

- ~ What are my wildest dreams, the ones I haven't dared to dream out loud?
- ~ If there were no limits or restrictions, what could I spend hours doing with a sense of joy in my heart?
- ~ What limiting beliefs, societal or otherwise, are causing me to dismiss the desires already living in my heart?

Dream the Dream

What does an illuminated future look like for you? What is it that conjures up light, excitement, and expansive feelings about your future? It can be as simple or as grand as you like – whatever suits your soul.

For some, it can be simple contentment, a happy, stable, and loving home environment where a family can flourish. Or your illuminated future might involve being the most confident version of yourself.

Take Action

When you have that five-year vision, the steps become clearer. For example, how can you bring more joy into your home? By decluttering, reducing screen time, improving nutrition, and spending more quality time with your family. Or how can you start bringing more love and acceptance to where you are now? Or taking those small but slightly uncomfortable steps out of your comfort zone so you can stretch the parameters of your fullest self?

When you allow yourself to explore that bigger-picture vision, new possibilities begin to emerge.

Pathways you may have never even considered start to appear in your field of awareness.

Then it's up to you to take aligned, intentional action to give dimension to those energetic pathways, and it's through that action that you breathe life into your highest timeline and bring it into being.

If you have a voice and a story that's calling to be shared, what opportunities can you find to connect with people who want to hear it? Connect with in-person community groups, start your own podcast, or share your voice on social media. The people you're looking for are looking for you, too.

Is your inner artist calling to be illuminated in your future? Get your materials, carve out time and space to prioritize your art, and channel your creativity.

If you have a call to start a passion-driven business that's more in line with your truth, what behaviors do you need to start shifting to take the steps to building and launching your business? Maybe it means ringfencing one sacred hour each week to plan, research, or, most importantly, act on your business dreams, even before you feel 'ready.'

Take the baby steps and build the momentum. Through your commitment, the outcomes will manifest. More on this in Chapter 13. For now, consider:

- If your illuminated life arrived tomorrow, would you be ready to receive it?
- If a big opportunity showed up, would you be ready to take it?
- If all the money were to show up in the morning, would you have a plan for managing it?
- If you want your dream home, are you making the most of the house you already have?
- If you want relationships where you're loved and respected, are you loving and respecting yourself?
- If you want to find more authentic and supportive friendships, where can you be a more authentic and supportive friend?

You don't have to be perfect or have it all worked out, just be willing to move from where you are to bring yourself into alignment with the energy of where you want to be.

It's time to start bringing your desires and truth into existence, my friend. It's time to let the universal energies light the tinder of your deepest soul truth.

Let the sparks of your soul catch fire and illuminate this world as you live out your wildest dreams.

It's time to expand your potential. Are you ready?

LIGHT ACTIVATION

Connecting with Your Illuminated Future

This Light Activation provides the foundation for you to connect with the frequency of your illuminated future. Don't worry if nothing comes through straight away – this activation is an initiation, an energetic opening into the realms of possibility. It will grow with you.

As your frame of reference expands, so will your possibilities. I recommend coming back to this practice, or at least its core principles, as frequently as you can to nurture the seeds of your illuminated future. Whenever you find a quiet moment, return to it. A great way to build it into your daily routine is to do it in the moments just before you fall asleep.

1. Your Future-Self Meditation

- Connect with the energy of your heart and, either quietly or out loud, open up the invitation:

'Soul, bring forward images of who
I really came here to be.'

- Now, take a deep, grounding breath. Become aware of the top of your head and feel, imagine, or visualize light pouring down through your crown and through your body.
- With each breath, this light builds in your heart space and begins to expand.
- As you settle into this, begin to sense or imagine an orb of light forming around you. With each breath, the vibration of the orb rises, its light growing in intensity.

- You're preparing to meet your future self, the version of you that's already living your illuminated life in full alignment with your soul's potential.
- Soon, you'll find yourself waking up, but not in this version of your life. You're about to wake up in the life that your soul is leading you toward.
- Visualize waking up in your future self's bed. How does the day begin?
- What kind of sheets are wrapped around you? What's the quality of the light in the room? What scents are in the air? What sounds do you hear? Look out of the window. What's your view? What do you do next? Head to the bathroom? Make a nourishing breakfast? Stretch or move your body gently? Pause at your altar in gratitude? What does your home feel like? Is anyone else there? What energy lives there?
- Now move through your day, remembering this is your future dream reality. What's on the agenda? How are you getting from place to place? Who are you spending time with and what's the quality of the conversations you're having? How are you generating income? What service, product, or offering flows from your heart to others?
- Let the details be rich. Feel the fabrics, notice the textures, bring all your senses into play.
- Let yourself feel the vibration of this life.
- Take a breath. Trust what comes, even if it feels far away or wildly different from your current reality.
- Breathe into it. Spend as much time within this creative space as you wish. Expand the vision as much or as little as you want – this is your space. The most important thing here is to do this often.

Through repetition, your soul will reveal your potential. Just be open and willing to receive, even if it feels wild and unattainable. Just trust the process, my friend.

2. **Set it Down on Paper**

- To close, take a moment to journal about your experience, noticing any themes that emerge, as well as any pictures, feelings, symbols, and key bits of information. Don't force anything, just flow with whatever energy is - or isn't - present.

- To conclude your journaling, write some creative 'I am' statements based on your experience, for example: 'I am in my joy.' 'I am embodying my creativity.' 'I am at one with the energy of my illuminated living space.' 'I am evolving the vision of what is possible.' And so it is.

....

CHAPTER 12

Build Your Community

'Don't allow yourself to be kept small by the projections of those who have yet to embrace their own light. Build a community that wants to see you shine, rejoices in your glow, and is inspired by your growth.'

When a caterpillar turns into a butterfly, it has a period in a cocoon that holds space for its transformation. Much of the work from the first two stages of this book takes us deep into our own cocoon. We often find ourselves in a hermit phase of our life, holding the energetic space to break down all that was so that we can emerge anew. And when we do emerge from our cocoon, we look different, perhaps not physically, but energetically. Like the caterpillar, we no longer inch along, our bellies dragging along the floor; now we emerge, wings spread, unrecognizable from the person we once were.

Can you imagine being that butterfly? Who have you become? Does your self-image have to catch up with you?

This chapter is about nurturing your surroundings to support your expansion.

A Shifting Sense of Community

Human connection is vital for our well-being; the right people and environments can energize our spirit and stoke our light. So, through this process, it's more important than ever to review your sense of community.

When you're on a journey of healing the past, activating your light, and deepening your spiritual connection, you might begin to find that what once offered you a sense of community and belonging no longer resonates with you in the same way. The places you used to frequent, the music you listened to, the narratives you soaked up, and the people you spent time with, just don't quite resonate in the ways they once did.

At this stage, you may be hearing your soul speak through intuitive nudges or breakdowns in relationships. Like the shifting of tectonic plates to realign you, it gives you the opportunity for reflection and the creation of space so that you can welcome in new resonant frequencies.

It's not just about the people you hang out with, or where you physically live, it's the creators whose content you absorb, the programs you watch, the belief systems you adopt, and the energetic containers you allow your energy to rest in.

For me, community is:

> **Community** (kəˈmjuː.nə.ti) *noun*
> The people, spaces, and places you come into energetic unity with. Come-unity.

A merging of energies that occurs through shared environments, physical or digital, belief systems, values, and interactions.

This means becoming discerning about your energy and seeking out ways to build on your community, so that it contributes to your growth and expansion rather than keeps you tethered in limitation.

Decisions and Boundaries

Some of us will be called to make tough decisions about whether everyone moves forward with us into the next stages of our lives. You'll need to determine what best serves your future mental, physical, and spiritual well-being.

As the saying goes, 'People are here for a reason, a season, or a lifetime.' The wisdom lies in knowing when the season has passed or when the reason or lesson has been fully received, and recognizing when it's time to shift or set up the appropriate boundaries.

There comes a time when we need to acknowledge that certain energies are no longer supportive, so that we may refocus our energy into the people, places, and activities that'll support us in becoming the best version of ourselves. We want to be in communities that expand the capacity and light of our heart chakra.

This doesn't mean going through your phone book and ditching all your friends and family in a dramatic break-up, it's just an invitation to really connect with your energetic response to your relationships.

Some relationships are just too toxic to repair. Some require firm boundaries in order for them to work effectively for both parties, but if you've been in an ongoing relationship with someone who's benefited from your previous lack of boundaries, then the transition to the implementation of your new boundaries isn't always going to be plain sailing.

When you've been an ever-giving source of emotional, energetic, or practical nourishment and then you implement boundaries and withdraw your energy, it will be felt. Imagine pulling out the IV line that's been keeping someone fed from your source. Of course, they'll notice its absence.

Implementing boundaries isn't always comfortable, but it's necessary. If you don't have firm boundaries, this in itself is a communication with our energetic universe that leaves you open to being energetically taken advantage of. You may well find yourself attracting people who're more than happy to suck from your metaphorical bosom until your supply becomes dry.

Not everyone is entitled to ongoing, unquestioned access to your energy. If you fail to put those boundaries in place, you're likely to find yourself in ongoing periods of frustration as the misalignment becomes too much to bear, and then you end up feeling resentful.

Now for a little bit of tough love, from a place of care...

You are responsible for what you give.

I know it's not always easy if you've been a perpetual people-pleaser in the past, but here comes the concept of radical self-responsibility again. Either you establish the boundary or you keep feeling the drag and the slow, exhausting drip of being energetically milked, over and over again.

Pick your discomfort: the discomfort of having an uncomfortable conversation quickly to establish boundaries, or the discomfort of being drained on an ongoing basis.

Change and Growth

In life, we go through phases, from school to workplaces and different social interests, and if we're living as our soul intends, we grow and evolve. And so do the people around us. But sometimes, the people around us don't grow, and they've no intention of doing so. And sooner or later, we begin to feel distance opening up between us as life takes us in different directions.

Not everyone has ambition, or an interest in changing or evolving in life. Some folk are unwilling to evolve and some are happy to just stay as they are, and it's not our job to drag them anywhere either, they have their own soul path and free will. 'You can take a horse to water but you cannot make it drink.' But that doesn't mean *their* contentment with staying where they are should inhibit *our* call to expand and grow.

Sometimes, we have amazing people in our community, but life's busy. Along come partners and children, as well as parents or grandparents who need care. People move to new locations, and it's not that we're out of alignment with them, it's just that we're busy with life, and when we come back together, it's all love like we never had a day apart. But, unless we're intentional about making those connection points to come back together, before we know it, it's been months or even years, and we haven't seen each other.

It can feel lonely when you commit to healing and soul growth, as you spend many hours sitting tender in your shadows and in reflection. It's easy to feel isolated, especially if you've experienced a spiritual awakening and the people around you haven't. You can end up feeling like a bit of an outlier at a time when you probably need that sense of community more than ever.

Also, in Western society, the sense of community has become more fragmented. With the change in social climate over the years, both parents are often forced to work to keep up with the cost of living, people are feeling the pinch of less disposable income, and almost everyone's tired, burnt out, and overstimulated by the barrage of information that comes through the small electronic devices we can barely keep out of our hands.

Life has moved online, and breakdowns in our sense of community were exacerbated by the pandemic, which further eroded in-person connection by enforcing isolation and social distancing. As a result, the world of hospitality and entertainment saw a decline that we've never quite bounced back from.

It's time to reconnect, it's time to be intentional about how, and with whom, you're investing your precious energy.

Energy Is Currency

Be wise about how you invest it – you don't want to be doing the energetic equivalent of going to the betting shop every morning to spend it on a bet that you're going to lose. You want to be making conscious choices about how to spend your energetic currency, opting to invest it in sources that nourish you back. Like spending money on a green juice that'll nourish you from the inside out versus a vodka and coke that'll leave you with an energetic hangover. Nourish yourself.

There's no better time to invest in connections that support your journey and elevate your energy than now.

Lean in to the people that lift you up, lean in to the people that support your ventures, lean in to the people that bring you joy, lean in to the people that support your expansion.

Notice those who watch but can't bring themselves to cheer, and don't sweat it, just notice and adjust your energy accordingly.

Seek out those who inspire you with wisdom. Seek out those whose stories resonate with you. Seek out those who stoke your creativity.

Seek out those who inspire you to take bolder steps, but also be willing to seek out those who keep it real, from a place of love. And I say 'a place of love,' because keeping it real without the loving intention often just lends itself as an opportunity to put someone down. If they keep it real but it doesn't offer a growth opportunity, is it compassionate feedback?

Some of my greatest growth has come from being in the company of people who push me to grow by challenging my patterns. When the challenge comes from a person who holds your best interests at heart and comes from a place of love and respect, lean in to that, too.

We don't need to surround ourselves with people who just tell us what we want to hear all the time. It's not about creating an echo chamber, because we need contrast to know our truth, too.

Aligning with truth doesn't always mean that we're ready to receive it. But when that truth is rooted in love, we can at least hold it gently, giving our defense systems time to soften and our nervous system space to recalibrate in response to what may initially feel like an attack. This is why it's important to be discerning about the people you have in your space and invite feedback from.

Let your inner circle be made up of those who honor your growth, people who speak with love even when it burns a little, and who remind you of your light when you forget it.

You don't need yes-people. You need people who can reflect what you need to see to help stretch you.

The right kind of community is one that holds compassionate space for your expansion.

Reflect on Your Community

Take a moment here to feel intuitively into your existing communities. Not just the people you speak to on a regular basis – your family, your friends, your neighbors – but the spaces you spend time in, whether online or in person. Bring forward the roles you play and the circles you sit in.

- Can you think of someone you know who always brings the good vibes, who always leaves you feeling inspired or energetically light?
- Can you think of a friend that you can trust with your darkest shame-stirring secret, knowing they will hold it lightly and with love, not judgment?
- Can you think of a person in your life who phones, and at the end of the conversion you know everything about what's happening for them and they know very little about what's going on for you? Be honest, who in your life consistently pulls your energy down?
- Can you think of a person who's quick to have someone's name negatively in their mouth?
- Can you think of a person who simply knows how to hold space for whatever you're moving through? Or a person you spend time with who perpetually lowers your vibration?
- Take a moment to tune in to how you feel energetically after your interactions. Do you leave feeling replenished or depleted?

- Do your closest relationships empower you, see you, and value your contribution? Is the exchange mutually nourishing?
- What about the spaces you enter where you see yourself reflected, or the containers that are filled with love and authentic energy?
- Where do you feel you can't be authentic?

As you grow and evolve, re-evaluate your relationships, your role within them, and the quality of the frequency that they hold. Establish boundaries where necessary.

You have every right to withdraw, reduce, or control access to your energy from places and people that perpetually deplete you. If you're in a situation where you can't just withdraw your energy, understand how it impacts you and double down on filling your bucket so that you can be more in control of how much energy you give away.

But what about you, how do you show up for others? Where can you do better? You don't want to bypass the role that you play.

A community isn't just a power source for us to take from, it's something we should be enriching as well. We're not just out there with long arms and short pockets, ready to extract and not put something back in. Like turning up to the cook-out with a plate but no dish to share. It's about what we contribute, not just what we can take away.

Take a moment to reflect on that, too.

Self-Inquiry Journal Prompts

Think of your community. Ask yourself:

- ~ What does community mean to me?
- ~ What do I need from it?
- ~ What do I bring to it?
- ~ What isn't always well-received by others?
- ~ What might I need to take responsibility for?
- ~ What communities do I want to connect more with?

Shadowy Relationships

As you develop your energetic sensitivity, you may also become increasingly sensitive to the energetic output of others. Social media is notorious for those monitoring spirits who seem to watch every story but never provide support or encouragement. They're just there stacking up views but sending no good energy your way.

When you begin to rise into your power and step out into your ventures, you may well come to find that there are folk in your sphere who were very happy when you were small, but as soon as you start to elevate your position, they just can't seem to bring themselves to cheer you on.

I speak to a lot of people who've been doing the deep work to transform their lives, and they could have literally walked through the pit of hell and come out the other side and there'd still be people who couldn't bring themselves to cheer for them. Having people who you love or who are close to you responding to your growth in this way can be disheartening.

But you aren't bound to their perceptions of you. Sometimes your light will cast shadows on others. It reveals their unresolved pain and where they are yet to stand in their light. It highlights their shadows, and if they're not quite ready to use their resistance as an impetus for growth, don't let those shadows keep you in the shade.

That's not your cross to bear, my friend. Have compassion for others, but don't dim your own light. You've worked so hard to claim it, let yourself bathe in its glow.

New Connections

Now that your frequency's shifting and you're realigning, it's time to go forth and find your people. Although they may not be visible yet, they're out there. And this is where you need to be willing to actively seek them out.

The more you step into your truth and authenticity, the more self-reflective you are, the easier it is to find resonant people, places, and spaces, and through the refinement of your spirit it's far easier to discern what's no longer for you on an energetic level.

So, be willing to step out of your comfort zone, get out there, and be the new person in the room. Find clubs and events that support your hobbies, interests, and goals. Join community circles. Go where your people are, and if you're not sure where that is yet, it's time to start feeling it out.

Browse websites like Eventbrite or your local equivalent to see what's going on that piques your interest. Join book clubs, supper clubs, mentoring schemes, or community groups. Join craft or art classes. Go to a group exercise class or mobilize behind a cause that you're passionate about. Or if accessibility is a challenge, find spaces online to lean in to. And if you're looking for a gentle, reflective, soul-nourishing space, join me in my Heart Healing and Soul Growth community. It's for women who are healing their past, activating their light, and rising into their potential together.

Whatever lights you up, makes you feel passionate, calls to your curiosity, or speaks to your soul, go forth into the world and connect with it.

Build your community!

LIGHT ACTIVATION

Go Forth and Connect

This week, I invite you to become intentional about the energy of community. Not just the people around you, but also the spaces your energy frequents, the voices you follow, the timelines you scroll through, and the conversations that you entertain day to day.

- Be aware of what you encounter that lowers your vibe or causes energetic irritation. These feelings could be providing you with an invitation to make adjustments. Don't forget, as you move through the week, that you get to choose how much energetic debt you're willing to carry from interactions that deplete you. You are the master of your resources.

So, let this be a week of energetic realignment:

- Curate your social feeds with what stokes a fire in your heart and energizes your inspiration. Unfollow who or what no longer resonates, and make room for creators who reflect the light you're stepping into.
- Seek out YouTube channels, podcasts, and spaces that uplift and inform, not dumb down or distract.
- And say 'yes' to real-world connections that feel nourishing and uplifting, not performative or draining. Follow up on those plans to catch up with the people that you want to spend more time with and in the process you can support your local independent coffee shop or juice bar. Boosting independent business and making human connections - everyone's a winner!
- Bring both your digital and physical environments into alignment with the light that you're becoming.

Your energy is precious and powerful. Spend it like the sacred currency that it is.

CHAPTER 13

Contraction and Expansion

'I trust that challenges and discomfort reveal opportunities for growth and healing, empowering my journey to wholeness and the deep magic of human expansion.'

Your magical life is opening up for you. Your energy, circles, and inner world are all shifting in your favor. This is the part of our light-activation journey that I refer to as 'the contraction and expansion cycle.'

We contract when fear and self-doubt kick in, we stretch when we lean in to the discomfort, and we expand when we move through it and find ourselves transformed on the other side.

Contraction

Through the process of activating your light, you're experiencing a rebirth. The contraction phase is a natural part of the birthing process. It's important to understand this now, so you're prepared when it occurs.

Having an awareness of it can prevent setbacks and help you to begin to trust that contraction is often an essential part of emerging into the light of a new timeline.

It's the tension before the stretch.

It's where you move beyond the predictable environment of your comfort zone and into the realms of your illuminated future by taking intentional action that supports your soul growth.

You've probably heard the phrase, 'Fake it until you make it.' But for me, it's less about faking and more about starting to embody the energy of your illuminated self, even before you feel fully ready. It might not sound as catchy, but it encapsulates the reality of the process better, because you're not faking, you're allowing your nervous system to gently adjust to a new frequency, one small aligned step at a time. You're showing yourself what's possible and creating safety in the stretch as you move in the direction of who you're becoming.

You've done the inner work, you've sat with the discomfort, you've called in the guidance, and now it's time to align the pipes and turn on the tap, because your light cannot flow if it's blocked by inaction.

Energies are lining up to support your expansion. They want to work with you and weave magic through your life, and you're required to meet those energies and opportunities with action.

If you're not willing to match the emotional and spiritual work with aligned action in the physical world, the energetic realms can only take you so far. So at this point you may have gained some wisdom, but wisdom without embodiment will keep you stifled and stuck in old ways of being, under the illusion of expansion.

You haven't come this far to hoard wisdom, you've made it this far because it's time to truly embody your illuminated self.

If you've spent many years within the predictable parameters of your patterns and routines, though, this stage can feel like a stretch.

The Stretch

For some, the stretch feels like a natural progression of healing, while for others, it can feel too much to bear, making them want to retreat to the safety of the familiar.

You may have heard the saying, 'You can't do what you've always done and expect to get different results.' If you want to get your illuminated future, it's time to do something different.

My friend, you're probably going to have to get a little uncomfortable. But think about it this way...

What's more uncomfortable in the long run? Staying stuck and feeling the frustration of restricting your light and never knowing what it's like to taste your illuminated future, or experiencing the temporary discomfort of taking a chance on something aligned with your highest vision for yourself?

Take a breath.

You don't have to go from being a recluse to dancing on tables tomorrow, there are many steps in between. But to achieve your transformation, you'll need to learn to work with and through the discomfort.

Soul growth occurs when you become clear about what you want for your life, step into your courage, and start making small shifts to embody the change.

Let me use myself as an example. I was agoraphobic, and today I share my story with others on camera and on stage, but I didn't go from being scared to go to the corner shop to speaking on stage, overnight. It was through a process of exposure. Or controlled experiments, if you will.

Strength comes through aligned exposure to the things that block or restrict the flow of our energy, inhibiting it from manifesting its potential.

The more action you take, the more feedback you receive, the more laser-focused you become, and the more you refine your actions, the more momentum and confidence you build. Confidence is built through action. Your solar plexus is strengthened through action.

So, at one point, my biggest fear was leaving the house. Can you guess what the antidote to that fear was? That's right, leaving the house.

My next challenge was to build my confidence so I could begin to share my story, but I was scared to talk on camera. So, what was the antidote? I pulled my phone out on the street and filmed myself, even if I was cringing and hugely uncomfortable.

And before each step I took, my brain tried to fire off all the reasons not to do it.

However, it was through this process of pushing through, despite the contraction, that I was able to achieve more audacious goals and meet more expanded versions of myself, which helped me connect with more aligned people.

Making Intentions

At the close of each year, I sit with my journal, connect with my guides, and set intentions for the year ahead. Not resolutions, *intentions*.

Through the process of being written into my journal, my intentions are cast out into the field of possibility, and the energies go to work.

One particular year, I set the intention to expand my network and increase my speaking opportunities. Public speaking had always been a big fear of mine, but I knew it was something I needed to face if I were truly going to succeed in my mission to connect with people and share inspiration, hope, and healing.

They say that when the student is ready, the teacher appears.

The following January, the teacher did appear, through lollipop mentoring and its incredible network of mentors.

lollipop is a dedicated mentoring community for Black women in the marketing and advertising industries, founded by the wonderful Maria McDowell. Through it, I was connected with people and opportunities that showed me, like nothing else, the truth of the contraction and expansion cycle.

This is why we discussed the importance of community in the previous chapter. At lollipop, I found women who saw me, believed in me, and wanted to see me succeed.

Through lollipop, I met mentors in Shaline Manhertz and Kristianah Fasunloye, strategic consultants who are passionate about supporting leaders to lead, and Lou Nylander, founder of the Wildflowers of London, a collective of professional women dedicated to networking, personal growth, and supporting women-owned businesses. These women would soon be presenting opportunities for me to overcome my fear of public speaking.

Lou invited me to speak at an event for her Wildflowers community. This would be my first paid public-speaking event. The evening was titled 'Flourishing through Challenges: The Road to Resilience with Zoe Fox.'

Eeeeeek. A whole audience and me?! My name on the event. No one else to hide behind. No panel. No team to work on edits before it went live. No rehearsal. Just me, my sweaty palms, my palpitations, my fear.

I knew I was being divinely guided to these opportunities for expansion.

After all, they were exactly what I'd asked for, but that didn't mean I wasn't petrified.

Every cell and every chakra wanted to contract. What if I fail, what if I freeze, what if my mouth dries up, what if I have a panic attack, or can't get my words out?

And honestly, what was I supposed to do as a disabled speaker? I *can* stand, but not comfortably or for long, and I worried that if I just sat on a chair, I wouldn't be engaging enough. I couldn't exactly pace about the stage or work the room, not with two elbow crutches clanking about awkwardly. I worried that my disabled body would become a barrier to creating engagement and connection with the audience.

And spinal cord injury brings its own set of challenges. What if my body embarrasses me, what if I have a bowel accident or a leg spasm mid-flow, what if I fall over, or pass wind in the silence? Spinal cord injury doesn't care who's in the room or where you are. From experience, I know that the body will do what it's going to do.

What if, what if, what if... each 'what if' contracting me tighter, like a boa constrictor working its way around my body. Every last possible fear and anxiety came up for review. I was sure I was going to spontaneously combust right there on the stage. My anxiety was doing its best to find every reason for me to make an excuse not to do it.

Still, I diligently prepared slides to present, covering every point I wanted to make – but the fear weighed heavily on me, following me all the way up to the event.

On the night, my mate Ruth came with me for some moral support, but the drive to the venue was a blur.

As everyone sat down, Lou guided me to a chair she'd thoughtfully arranged for me. I sat down, took a deep breath, and let myself imagine roots anchoring me to the earth, helping me feel more grounded.

The next thing I knew, I was being introduced, and then the spotlight was on me. Slides loaded. But as I looked out at the audience, at a group of women, just like me really, sitting open and ready to listen, I felt a little more at ease.

And so I began... and once I did, they couldn't shut me up. I think I went through three slides before sharing my life story with everyone, as if we were besties on a girls' night in. Then the church bells at St Ethelburga's, where the event was being held, started chiming, and one of the team gently signaled that I only had a few minutes left. *Wait, what? My slides!* We didn't even get to the meditation I'd planned. I'd somehow talked my way through a full 60 minutes, and I'd barely stopped to catch a breath.

When my time was up, I felt completely exposed, wondering if I'd spent an hour sharing the deepest parts of my life without offering anything of real value to the audience.

Afterward, I mingled with the ladies in attendance over drinks and a grazing board, and I heard women reflecting back to me their own traumatic and painful experiences.

Doing It Anyway

It was here that two things became clear:

1. I now had a basis on which to refine my public speaking and make right the things I wanted to improve on next time.

2. Human connection came through visibility and vulnerability.

From there, speaking opportunities flowed. Shaline, Kristianah, and Lou lined up more for me. Now I knew I just needed to be prepared, take a breath before I began, and hold on to my intention to connect and inspire.

Do my palms still get sweaty? Yes. Does anxiety still rise? Definitely. However, I now have real-life reference points for what's possible when you work through the contraction.

With each opportunity, it becomes a little less scary, and you become a little more confident in your capabilities. No doubt this will be the same for you, too. The first step may feel scary, but from there, your nervous system begins to trust that you can handle it, and even better, that you can exceed your own expectations.

Be prepared to meet and move beyond your resistance. Be prepared for the stretch. The stretch is where the magic happens, it's the point between who you've been and who you're becoming.

Below are some examples of how this might be showing up in your own life right now.

If you've been afraid to speak up...

Your stretch might involve sharing your opinion in a meeting, posting authentically online, or expressing your true feelings to someone. Your contraction might feel like making excuses or putting it off.

If you've kept your dreams quiet...

Your stretch might be saying them out loud for the first time or writing them in your journal as if they're already real. Or researching that course, business idea, or retreat you've been dreaming about. Your contraction might look like dismissing your dreams and shutting them down, as well as noticing resistance to committing to them.

If you've always taken care of others and neglected yourself...

Your stretch might involve choosing rest over productivity, saying 'no' and implementing the boundaries we discussed in the last chapter, or deciding to ask for help, even if it makes you feel vulnerable. Contraction might appear as fearing upsetting someone and prioritizing their needs over your own.

If you're feeling underappreciated or undervalued at work...

Your stretch might be going for a promotion or leaving your job. Contraction might feel like making excuses about why it's better to stay put and not take the action, or questioning whether you're good enough at all.

If you've been hiding because of pain or trauma...

Your stretch might be showing up in the discomfort. Booking that healing session, making an appointment with a therapist, or taking the class or course you've always wanted to attend. Contraction might look like prioritizing something or someone else, making yourself busy, or finding other things you need to spend money on.

Imagine if you just took the action. Imagine if you made the move or took a chance on something different.

I mean, what's the worst that could happen?

These are some of the common fears I hear coming up:

What if no one likes it? What if it's not good enough? What if people judge me? What if I fail? What if I look stupid? What if I waste my time, money, or energy? What if it doesn't work?

It's true that:

You might try something and it doesn't go as planned.

You might get rejected. You might feel embarrassed. You might cry. You might have to start again. You might not receive the celebration, support, or validation you hoped for.

However, you'll gain the opportunity to reflect and refine, and have the chance to be even more authentic and intentional when you take your next steps.

Remind yourself that it's okay. Life isn't perfect, but if it were, we wouldn't have these beautiful opportunities to stretch, learn, grow, reassess, and redefine what really matters to us.

If it doesn't go to plan, learn from it.

If you get rejected, there may be a greater plan unfolding.

If you feel embarrassed, can you trust that it will pass?

If you have to start again, can you see it as an opportunity to build anew with even more authenticity and even deeper resonance with your illuminated self?

These are all beautiful opportunities, and when you view them in this light, the resistance becomes much more manageable to work with. Which brings us to...

Working Through Resistance

To work with contraction energy and into expansion, it helps to be aware of your resistance. If you're not aware of it, you might believe it, and stop your expansion before you've even truly begun.

Self-sabotage can be so automatic that you can dismiss an opportunity for expansion before it's even had a chance to land in the energetic field of possibility. Because the pattern is in place so quickly, you might not even notice how you automatically discount opportunities:

- You start to convince yourself you're not ready.

- You get lost in perfectionism, telling yourself you just need to complete one more course, earn one more certificate, or make one more tweak before you're qualified enough to move forward.
- You start to make up excuses.
- You find yourself procrastinating. Suddenly you have an urgent need to start tidying up rather than working on your dream or vision.
- You start to compare yourself to people on Instagram and convince yourself you're not good enough yet.

In addition to the mind, the body can also become involved in resistance. The palpitations step up, you feel tense and anxious, your throat gets sore, or you find yourself needing a nap just thinking about doing the thing you're being called to do, because the resistance energy is overwhelming.

It's a self-protection strategy, getting your excuse in before you fail, stopping yourself before you've even begun, because the fear of failure is so unbearable.

When you see this come into play, see it for what it is: the contraction before the expansion.

Contraction Check-in

At points of contraction, ask:

- Is this helping me to heal?
- Is this supporting my growth?
- Is this helping me expand my creative expression?

- Is this helping me show up in my truth and authenticity in the name of the greater good?

If the answer is 'yes,' it can help you take that courageous action, which, granted, might take you out of your comfort zone and make you a little scared, but ultimately is in the name of honoring your expansion.

....

Expansion

The magic happens when we allow ourselves the grace to get to know ourselves in the discomfort of the expansive opportunities that invite us to grow. So, find comfort in the contraction, knowing it's the route to your expansion.

Your Energy Anchor

For support in finding comfort in your expansion, it can be really helpful to identify an energy anchor and use this as your compass. An energy anchor is a thing that operates as your 'why', aka your purpose, your reason, your motivation.

Your energy anchor could be :

- To heal generational trauma for your lineage and redefine possibilities for future generations.
- To feel present and safe in your body.
- To live life with more meaning by sharing your gifts, heart, or art with others.
- To live fully authentically in line with your soul's truest expression.

- To be financially free while remaining in integrity with your values.
- To inspire others and support their healing by showing what's possible through your own.
- To be the representation you always dreamed of.

It might be one or more of the above, or something entirely different, or perhaps it's all still taking shape and settling into your field as a result of the deep work you've been doing.

Whatever your energy anchor is, let it be the thing that keeps you steady in the storm and the compass that guides you toward your destination.

When you're clear about what your energy anchor is, taking action becomes easier. The steps begin to reveal themselves. Boundaries become easier to honor. And your reason for moving through the contraction shines like a light at the end of the tunnel, a light so bright and deeply desired by your soul that eventually you come to find comfort in the contraction itself, grounded in the deep trust that it's leading you toward your expansion.

LIGHT ACTIVATION

Moving Through Contraction

Here, you'll discern and illuminate your resistance, using your journal to support you as you move through the contraction stage. It can be helpful to bookmark this activation for when you encounter resistance and find yourself in the contraction space.

1. **Inner Resistance**

- As you become aware of inner resistance, find a place where you won't be disturbed.
- Take a deep breath in to bring your energy within.
- Set the intention to learn from and grow beyond any resistance you encounter on the path to realizing your highest potential.

2. **Breaking Through**

Imagine your contracted, resistant self standing on one hand and your illuminated self standing on the other. You might like to do this as a visualization or write out the two parts on paper.

- Spend a moment with each version of yourself. What do you notice about each one?
- Imagine each of them standing in a cloud of energy. Notice the qualities of the energy - the color, vibrancy, texture, and density.
- Which hand feels lighter?
- Which version of yourself feels more magnetic to you?
- What does the contracted resistant self want to say to the illuminated self?
- What does the illuminated self want to say to the contracted self?
- Imagine each version has a message for you. What do they have to say?
- Thank each of them for their insights.

3. Expansion

- Spend a moment visualizing the light of your illuminated self expanding. It starts by encompassing your entire hand, then it expands to surround your whole body.
- Now, breathe in that light. On the exhale, visualize exhaling the colored energy of the small contracted self. Every in-breath fills you with the energy of illumination, and every exhale releases the energy of your contracted self.
- Continue this breathing cycle until the contraction energy is expelled, and your illuminated energy is also expressed on the exhale.
- Close with a breath to integrate the activation.

Take a few moments to journal about your experience. What did you learn? How did you feel before the exercise? How do you feel now?

Return to this Light Activation anytime the resistance rises to support yourself in moving through your contraction into the stretch and out into your expanded self.

. . . .

CHAPTER 14

Shine Your Light

'Shine – like humanity depends on it.'

Take a breath. You've made it this far. What a great testimony to your curiosity, character, and sense of possibility. And your consistency. That'll take you far. It's in the roots of that consistency that you can anchor *any* transformation or change that you want to see in your life.

Before we wrap up this journey, this final chapter invites you to shine your light, and as you do, you'll take stock of the inner transformation you've journeyed through and give thanks for how far you've come. You'll explore expanding further, as well as how to stay aligned and anchored when setbacks arise and to trust in divine timing.

But this isn't just a healing journey, it isn't just about personal transformation and self-centered desires. This is about activating the light in our world, one soul at a time. It isn't just a solitary quest, it's an audacious invitation to transform the world as we know it.

So, you'll also explore how to embody your light in tangible ways by making empowered choices that support your highest path and contribute to activating more light in the world around you.

You could say this is where personal transformation meets collective impact, on a mission that is far greater than us as individuals.

Embody Your Truth

It's time for you to integrate your authenticity and embody the expansion that first spoke to you in a whisper – embody the deepest truths and aspirations that have been rumbling in the depths of your being.

It's time to be the architect, the builder, and to move forward as the driver, seated firmly in the potential of your soul, as you bring your dreams and visions into manifestation in the physical realm.

You've taken back control of your story, your narrative, and your energy. You've activated your spiritual magnetic essence, and now you're bringing consciousness and intention into the ways you carve out your days.

You've been cultivating self-awareness and mastery throughout this journey. The shifts you've been making *are* changing the trajectory of your life for the better. But this is a process, so have patience and please persevere through the moments when it feels like nothing's changing. It can take time to see the inner results reflected in your outer world. Trust that the universe is realigning things and it'll only be a matter of time before the tender green shoots of evidence of the shift in your inner world begin to show externally as well as internally.

A shift in awareness starts out like a tiny snowflake. With each intentional step that you take in line with your expanding awareness, your snowflake gathers others and grows into a small snowball. As it grows, it gains momentum. And with momentum comes movement. With movement comes transformation.

Whatever that illuminated future looks like for you, it's already on its way, and you're aligning with it through the action that you're taking to make it happen.

Give Thanks

You are who you are today because of what you've grown through. Take a moment to give thanks to the versions of yourself that survived through their pain to carry you here today.

Now look to the future, to who you're becoming.

And then bring it all back into this present moment of conscious creation and anchor it in with a breath.

Giving Thanks Meditation

- Take a moment in this breath to see yourself standing on the hump of an energetic bridge, one that stretches from your past into your illuminated future.
- As you glance back, acknowledge the murky soup of past pain, uncertainty, and challenge that you've emerged from, now distilled into a rich reduction, potent and deeply nourishing. This rich stock provides the basis for you to add more nourishment to the pot of your life as you shimmer into your future.
- Congratulate yourself. Through stepping into this invitation to activate your light, you've repaired wounded and weathered pathways, tenderly mending the road so that your light could, again, travel unhindered through your being, restoring you to the light you always were.

- You've let go of the baggage, shifted the stagnancy, and put yourself through a process of filtration to give your soul self a chance to shine.
- Give thanks to the soul pull that brought you here.

....

I'm curious to know what you feel has shifted within you. What are you more aware of now than before you started this book? What have you been able to nurture, grow, or begin to embody through this process?

Think about it and let it land with a breath. Do you feel your roots growing deeper? Can you feel your spine straightening with the energy of clarity that's downloading from your soul, through your crown chakra, as you embody your truth?

That's the beauty of this work: you become more rooted. More connected. More secure in who you are.

And from that grounded place, it becomes easier to act on intuitive nudges with decisiveness and courage, even when lingering limitations from the past want to pull you backward.

Expand Your Light

Courageous one, it's time to stretch beyond your comfort zone and into your expansion. It's time to dream beyond your dreams and push the boundaries of your vision.

How good can life get?

How peaceful can life get?

How abundant can life get?

How much fun can life be?

Can you feel the expansion in those questions? Ignite the light of your curiosity, expand the scope of these possibilities.

When you reach toward your potential through curiosity and intentional action, even when it's imperfect and you're not fully clear or confident, it carries a powerful opportunity to learn, explore, refine, grow, and expand more fully into the light of who you came here to be.

Hold Appreciative Space

I encourage you to hold appreciative space for your lessons and the opportunities that help you to grow, and acknowledge them with the respect they deserve. Mark your milestones and achievements, regardless of how big or small they may be.

A great way to do this is to have a jar, and each time you have something to acknowledge or celebrate, write a small note, fold it up, and add it to your jar. At the end of the year, before you set your intentions for the year ahead, review your jar and remind yourself of just how much you've achieved. Whether you're celebrating finally posting your first video online, stepping up into your activism, attending a new in-person community, spending less time doom-scrolling on your device, connecting with someone, gaining a new subscriber, or whatever it may be for you, note it, celebrate it, and give thanks for it. Let that gratitude amplify your light.

Stay Aligned

Remember, the path isn't linear. Not every day will feel high-vibe. You'll experience waves of expansion and contraction, flow and pause. It's all part of the great rhythm of life.

At times, signs, synchronicities, and intuitive nudges can feel like they're on an electric roll, popping up left, right, and center on a high-vibe wave. You'll find yourself meeting new people and being aligned with synchronistic and undeniable opportunities to say 'yes.'

Or you might find yourself coming across concepts that excite you, followed by an inner call to action.

Seize those moments, while being aware of your secondary resistance. I say 'secondary' because the immediate response will be a 'yes' or a zing of excitement before your patterns are triggered and start to find excuses and reasons to say 'no.' In time, old patterns will fade as you continue to take courageous, aligned action. With the new evidence that emerges from your willingness to move forward, you'll come to expect new, more favorable outcomes.

At other times, you might feel completely alone, questioning whether your guides are even there at all, doubting the magic of the universe, and leaning in to thinking that you're delusional.

Don't become despondent. Hold the faith. Don't let this be an excuse to give up and fall back into old habits.

In those moments when it feels like there's distance between you, the signs, the magic, and your guides, be intentional about staying in integrity. Keep walking in alignment. Be the embodiment of your light. Don't only show up when the signs are flowing, show up anyway. Let this be a way of life.

Sometimes, when you seem to be in a state of disconnection or challenge, actually you're in a pause between breaths, a stage of realignment, a transition between timelines. Hold your trust, maintain patience, and keep moving forward, taking action in alignment with your highest timeline.

Let the Greater Plan Unfold

When signs and opportunities do appear and your intuitive nudges are guiding you into action, try your best not to attach to specific outcomes. Even when exciting and seemingly aligned opportunities present themselves, it doesn't necessarily mean *your* desired result is the one that will manifest. When we pin our expectations to outcomes, we can end up disappointed. But sometimes, the real value, the true lesson, is revealed in what unfolds when things don't go according to our plan.

So, detach from trying to control the outcome and instead focus on taking those courageous, aligned steps that your intuition, curiosity, and guides are pulling you toward, and on finding the magic, wisdom, and enjoyment in all the steps along the way.

You'll inevitably meet with setbacks. It's par for the course. If you apply for a job and don't get it, if you make plans for a date and it doesn't turn out how you hoped, if you launch a business and it doesn't take off, if you make a proposal and it's rejected, don't resist your disappointment.

Don't swallow it down and pretend it didn't hurt, or it didn't matter. Feel it. Sit with your feelings. Acknowledge what's coming up for you. Look honestly at what that opportunity represented to you, and what you feel you lost when it didn't work out. Your emotions are often a powerful sign that the opportunity mattered to you. Don't deny them. But still, try not to doubt the process. Let the intelligence of divine timing unfold.

Can you allow yourself to trust divine timing? Can you trust that what isn't manifesting in your vision is in service of a greater plan?

We can get so attached to what we want, how it should look, and when it should happen. But often we're constructing our possibilities from a limited frame of reference and forgetting that we live in an infinite universe of infinite possibilities.

Control what you can. Don't waste your precious energy trying to force and control outcomes that are outside of your control.

Reflect and Realign

When the challenges come and things don't unfold in the way that you hoped, let them be invitations to pause, reflect, and gently realign. Each one holds the potential to deepen your trust in yourself, your path, and your ability to move forward with courage, clarity, and grace.

When you find yourself being bashed about by life's inevitable waves, it's a time to double down on your self-care. When the world feels out of control, bring your power back to what *is* in your control: the choices you make, moment by moment, to return to your light and anchor your roots.

Come back to the present. Come back to the parts of this book you bookmarked. Come back to the practices. When you feel out of control, come back to your breath, your journal, your altar, and the nourishment of your mind, body, and soul.

Be aware of your energy and what you need. Be it rest, be it a good cry, an ear, community, inspiration, whatever it may be, advocate for what you need. But most importantly, give yourself grace.

When the waves have receded, just check in with yourself and ask, 'What can I learn from this?'

Once you've licked your wounds and held space for the energy of disappointment or sadness, come back home to yourself.

Come back to the present. Honor the light you've worked so hard to reclaim by rising back into it.

The Ripple Effect

It's our sacred and societal duty to shine. When we step out courageously and authentically, with our light leading, we touch others.

Whether you realize it or not, your energy leaves an imprint. Your light matters. By being in your glow and standing in your heart-centered power, you increase the light and love on the planet.

I know it might feel like a single drop in the ocean, but even a single drop creates a ripple effect in the wider body of water.

Be the droplet, make a splash.

We live in a world that's in pain; it can be like looking out at a cloak of darkness shrouding our planet. Humanity is crying out for healing, and so many of us don't know where to begin. Feeling helpless, we sit behind our screens, witnessing tragedy and injustice unfolding in real time. We shout into our digital echo chambers, frustrated by how little seems to change.

But you aren't powerless, my friend. Do you hear me?

You are powerful. Your light carries with it the frequency of change. This world is calling out for more love, more compassion, more heart-centered humans like you, who are healing and standing fully in their power and light.

When we heal our wounds and societal conditioning, we come to see the humanity in one another. We stop seeing 'other' and discover more that connects us. We have been conditioned to be divided and ruled, and it suits some people to keep us that way, but when we come together in our light and collaborate, organize, and stand for the greater good, everything changes.

It's easy to feel overwhelmed by the events in the world, and our pain can feel too big to manage. But from this position of helplessness, we misplace our frustration, and we end up projecting our rage and grief outward and fueling the very energies that we long to dissolve.

It's time to channel smart.

If we want to birth a world rooted in healing and change, we need to mobilize behind healing and hope.

Radical Self-Responsibility

When we stop waiting for a savior or outside force to fix it all and instead embody radical self-responsibility and turn inward to confront our own pain, we no longer project our pain onto others. We begin to contribute from love. Because when we heal, when we awaken, we start to make conscious choices that serve not just our life, but the greater good.

Contribute your voice and light to the greater good. Use your voice to amplify truth, healing, and justice, and use your light to advocate for the voiceless.

We can all make conscious decisions about where our energy flows, from our time and attention to our money and actions.

See your spending as an energetic vote in favor of the kind of world you wish to see. Support small, independent, ethical local businesses. Pull power back from mega-corporations.

Let your choices reflect your values, even in small and everyday ways. It can be as simple as double-checking if the source of your avocado is an ethical one. Every conscious act is a move toward a shift for the greater good.

Where possible, divest from industries that exploit people and the planet. Shift your shopping choices, banking, investments, and your pension pot away from systems that fund war and injustice.

Turn away from anything that operates from a basis of fear, hatred, and division. Resist feeding the darkness. It's time to close down the energy supplies and stop feeding the sources that don't nourish a loving humanity.

Get behind political leaders and community groups that offer real hope from compassionate hearts, and if what you want to see isn't reflected there, be that change.

You can even start your own grassroots movement of like-minded souls. Whether it involves collective healing, local politics, organized resistance, or another cause that you care about that supports the greater good of Mother Earth and her people, unite in heart-led intention.

Mobilize in your light.

Lead with a loving, radiant heart to a brighter future.

When we act from our light, we tap into the healing potential of humanity. When we walk in our power, we inspire others to do the same. When we rebel against the status quo, when we shift away from the herd and root into our own vision, creating from our truth and from love, we inspire others to follow their dreams. When we model self-love, compassion, and courage, our children learn to do the same.

You'll find that when you shine your light, you broadcast a frequency of possibility that will invite your friends and family to explore their own potential. Even strangers you cross paths with will feel the warmth of your light, and it may well spark a reminder in them, too, that we aren't as disconnected as we've been led to believe.

Be in your power and give yourself
permission to follow what lights you up.

The healing of this planet begins with one awakened soul at a time. And you, my friend, are part of that change.

Whether your light is bright, fierce, warm, or soft, the future of Mother Earth and her children needs it all. Just let there be light, in your own unique form.

I used to carry the weight of the world on my shoulders, desperate to fix everything. My dad tried to ease the burden, reminding me that I couldn't heal the world alone. And he was right.

But now, here you are, too, doing this work, being active about being the light.

And together, we *can* make a difference.

This is *our* world. It's time to reclaim it.

It's time to reshape it through conscious choices, healed hearts, and awakened minds.

May your light ripple out through the world and restore the balance.

Darkness cannot withstand the light.

Take a breath. Claim your light.

LIGHT ACTIVATION

Shine Your Light

Redefine who you are in this world, on your terms, in your vision.

You've glimpsed your potential. You know you're a magnetic, energetic being. Now it's time to project that light into the world. Stop waiting for permission. Stop waiting for a savior. Stop waiting to be seen. Stop waiting for opportunities and start creating them. Be active in the curation of your illuminated life.

You're ready to shine your light, and you don't need permission!

Enter the conversations. Build the tables. Start the communities. Start telling people who you are and what you stand for. Project forth your soul-led vision and cast your magic out into the world. As you do, you amplify your magnetism and support the universe in aligning you with the right people, places, and opportunities.

Have you ever stopped to think about the word 'spelling'? Spell-ing. Your words are powerful. As you cast them onto paper and profiles, know that you're projecting an energy of potential and manifestation.

Redefine yourself to the world. Speak it. Spell it out. Weave your magic through your words. Update your bio. Rework your LinkedIn. Reintroduce yourself. Let the world meet the luminous, soul-led version of you.

Make a Personal Declaration

There's time for some final self-reflection before we close out. Answer the following questions and write your 'I am' statements in the present tense. Let them be a powerful declaration of your highest potential. Spell it out and activate that energy.

- Who are you? For example, 'I am... confident, assertive, compassionate, grounded, joyful, creative, resilient.'
- What qualities do you embody now? For example, 'I embody... self-love, courage, authenticity, kindness, inner peace, strength.'
- What do you stand for? For example, 'I stand for... equity, healing, love, freedom, integrity, truth, connection.'
- What impact do you wish to make on the world, your family, or your community? For example, 'I make an impact by... being the representation I want to see, inspiring others to heal, creating safe spaces, breaking generational cycles, embodying emotional availability, empowering communities.'

This is a dynamic statement. It will evolve as you grow. You can check back in every six months or at the end of the year and write a new statement. You can even write it on a sticky note and stick them layer on layer. It will be a lot of fun to look back over it and see how you're bringing this energy into manifestation.

Let this statement empower you to take conscious steps toward your illuminated future.

....

LIGHTWORK

Activate Your Wings of Light

Find a quiet place where you can be comfortable without interruption.

Close your eyes and take a few deep breaths, allowing your body to relax more deeply with every exhale and bringing your energy within.

1. **Ground Yourself**

- Become aware of your connection with the earth beneath you. Imagine roots beginning to grow down from the base of your spine or the soles of your feet. These roots can also extend from any other part of your body that feels natural and comfortable.

- Visualize these roots gently and lovingly penetrating the earth, reaching deeper and deeper until they connect to a large crystal at the core of Mother Earth.

2. **Enter the Temple of Light**

- Imagine yourself standing at the entrance of a majestic crystal cave. The cave is filled with a shimmering light that dances off the crystal walls. Take a moment to be still and appreciate the beauty before you. Notice the colors and textures, and feel the energy of the crystals amplifying your own energy.

- Begin to walk into the cave, each step taking you closer to a central chamber with a small opening at the top where you can see the mesmerizing glow of distant galaxies.

- As you enter this chamber, you notice a gentle pull upward, a sensation of high vibration and elevation. Your energy begins to rise, and you feel your body floating upward toward the opening, guided by a loving and comforting unseen force.

- As you rise, you're drawn toward the starry cosmos, feeling the vastness of the ever-expanding universe around you. You're lifted higher and higher until you find yourself before a magnificent Temple of Light, an enticing structure that radiates pure divine energy.

- As you approach the large, inviting doors of the Temple of Light, you place your hand on the door handle. Notice what it feels like under your palm and feel the warmth of the soft glow that seeps through the cracks of the doors.

- You open the doors and step inside the grandest ceremonial room you can picture. It's filled with an angelic light that streams through its great windows.

- In the center of the room, you see a circle of light on the floor, calling you to step into its warmth. You rest there for a moment, absorbing the frequency of the temple.

3. **Divine Connection**

- You feel a loving, gentle, but powerful presence behind you. Turning slightly, you see a group of 12 beings of light forming an archway with six beings positioned on each side. Their radiant love and supportive energy envelop you in a light-filled cocoon of divine love.

- The energy beckons you to walk through the archway. As you do, you feel the activation from each being of light as you pass them by. Their energies heighten your vibration and fill you with a sense of divine purpose and remembering. Your energy body is activated and uplifted with each step.

- As you emerge on the other side of the archway, you are bathed in a brilliant, comforting light. You feel its warmth on your back, like the soothing kiss of the sun.
- One of the light beings steps forward and places their hands on your shoulders. As they do so, you feel a powerful activation within you. An energetic crystalline wing structure begins to unfurl from your back, so light and vibrant, it feels ethereal.
- Take a moment to stretch and experiment with your new wings of light. Feel their high vibration and the sense of freedom they bring. You're now ready to fly with the confidence and grace of your true and highest self.
- The being of light communicates with you telepathically, imparting wisdom and reassurance. You understand that you have cleared the debris of your past and activated your inner light and are now ready to step onto your highest path.
- You absorb this sense of readiness with a deep breath in as you begin to bring your awareness back into your physical body. Gently make some small movements in a way that helps you to reconnect with your body. Feel your connection with the earth grounding you. Know that your wings of light are always with you, ready to support you on your journey to becoming your highest self.
- Take a deep breath into your belly to anchor in your light.

4. Embrace Your New Light

- Gently open your eyes, carrying with you an energy of empowerment and divine connection. You're ready to fully embody the transformative journey you've undertaken, to shine your light brightly, and to embrace the new possibilities that await you.

- So be it, so be it, and so it is.

A Final Note

You've come so far, special soul, and yet this is only the beginning.

Let these words meet you like a huge celebratory hug. I'm so grateful to you for showing up – for your inner child, for your future self, your present self, and humanity. Thank you for choosing to be a light that this world so desperately needs.

If this book has touched or supported you in any way, please share it with a friend and activate this global healing revolution.

I'd love nothing more than to see you light up the world as you continue your journey. Whenever you feel called to do so, share your moments, reflections, and breakthroughs using #ActivateYourLight on social media, and please feel free to tag me @zoeellenfox so we can contribute to the collective glow and inspire others to rise and shine in their own special way. Join my Heart Healing and Soul Growth community or sign up to my mailing list: www.zoefox.co.uk.

I wish you all the blessings, and send you all the love.

Go forth and *shine*, my friend. Be the light you want to see.

Big love,

Zoe xx

Acknowledgments

Thank you to:

Shola. My child, my teacher. You inspired me to grow, to dream bigger, and shine brighter so I could illuminate pathways for you. I love you, my baba. You bring light and expansion in all of us.

Kane, thank you for how you held the pieces of my broken heart, and supported me as I found the strength to place them back together. I will always be grateful for the role you played in helping me become the woman I am today.

Mama and Daddypops, thank you for this beautiful life. For your presence, your nurturing, the laughter, the memories, and for holding me in your love throughout my life.

My little bro, James, you've been there through every season and seen the most versions of me. Thank you for always believing in me and encouraging me into my potential, through Digital Group Media and beyond. Love you.

Uncles Ron and Pete, so blessed to have you, your presence, your wisdom, your love. Love you.

Aunty Anne, Aunty Louise, Uncle H, Joe, and Dan for your eternal love and support.

Joshua, Finley, Jessica, Jacob, Archie, Nyah, and Elijah. May you reach for the stars and discover the magic of who you are and what you're capable of.

My loved ones in spirit:

Grandad Lewis, who showed me a love like no other.

Granny Theresa, for loving me beyond the veil and helping me to glimpse the world of spirit with your presence.

Grandad Norm, with his healing hands and signposts from spirit.

Granny Eve, who showed me the power of connection as she transitioned this life with such grace.

Aunty Lynda, and it's from the old we travel to the new, keep me traveling along with you.

G.O.D., a short life that burned fast and bright. Thank you for the lessons.

Honorable mention to the one and only Collette Warren, who stood by me in friendship even when I'd lost myself. Through the dark shadows, the wild adventures, the laughter, the love, and the private jokes. You dance like a rocket, 'Claudette.'

Special love to Hayley B., Hayley J., Ruth, Tara, and Sandra for your consistent love, encouragement, and presence. Beautiful humans, your light is a gift to humanity.

Naomii, Keira, Sandi, Yazzie, and all the incredible women that I get to call my friends. I'm grateful for your love and support.

My Colihaut family, Val, Edith, Olivia, Sharlyne, Elenie, and Junior and the extended family.

K, aka Krust, my mentor, thank you for helping me break through the blocks that once held me back and move forward with clarity and confidence. And Ross and the Adapt the Canvas gang for riding the waves over the years.

Kerry and Young Urban Arts Foundation for taking a chance on me, entrusting me with leadership, and reminding me I was made for more when corporate life crushed my worth. And thank you for donating this MacBook on which I write.

My wider Junglist family, with honorable mention to Deman Rocker. Keep shining.

Thank you to the entire Hay House family:

Louise Hay, for creating this magical publishing company, and Reid Tracy, for driving it forward.

Michelle Pilley. In a world where I was constantly told to be less of myself, you invited me to be more. And here we are. Thank you.

Kezia Bayard-White, my commissioning editor, and Grace Rahman, my editor, thank you for your guidance and encouragement.

Cathy Levy and Lizzie Henry for your support and thoughtful reflections in the final polish of the manuscript.

Jessica Huie for founding the Diverse Wisdom program and amplifying voices that need to be heard.

Sophie Bashford for your wisdom, mentorship, and divine space-holding.

All the authors who shared their time and wisdom: Suzy Ashworth, Rebecca Campbell, Dr David Hamilton, Kyle Gray, Sonia Choquette, Dr E.

Farah Orths for walking every step with me, and for truly teaching me how to receive. The richness of your friendship and your holding through life is so precious. You are precious.

Madeline McQueen for the encouragement and empowerment, and for reminding me of my worth.

Valerie Richie, the Crone Goddess, a powerhouse of strength, courage, and wisdom.

Sasha Archer, Natasha Page, Kreena Dhiman, and the entire Diverse Wisdom cohort.

lollipop mentoring and Maria McDowell, thank you for helping me step out of my comfort zone, believe in my power, explode my opportunities, and expand my network.

Shout-out to Lou Nylander and the Wildflowers of London community.

Shaline Manhertz, Kristianah Fasunloye, and Karen Charles for your encouragement.

Jamelia Donaldson and the Treasure Tress team for the representation, the magic you create, and for celebrating me.

Aisha Deeply Rooted, Nai Wynter, and Zeena Edwards, thank you for being my original IG cheerleaders, and to our beautiful Nina Lopes, rest ever peacefully.

Dearest Bella Clark for your healing support, synchronistic magic, and for expanding my energy work through the realms of Pranic Healing. You're a powerful healer with a beautiful heart.

The late Master Choa Kok Sui, for your teachings, and Les Flitcroft, for sharing them with the world.

My Ladbroke Grove community. No community like it. Justice for Grenfell ♥

The divine source of creation for this magical experience called life, and my spirit team for cutting through the noise with your guidance.

The organizations that supported me on this path:

The Spinal Injuries Association

The London Spinal Cord Injury Centre, Stanmore

Horatio's Gardens and Aspire

The wider SCI community

And last but not least, thank *you*, beloved reader, for buying this book, for trusting the calling, and honoring the whisper that tells you you're here for more.

About the Author

Zoe E. Fox is a writer and intuitive guide devoted to helping women heal, elevate their energy, and step into their soul's potential. Her work is shaped by lived experience, spiritual connection, and years of studying metaphysics, counseling psychology, and energy work. Through her heart-led healing sessions and workshops, Zoe supports women in transforming old patterns and reclaiming their light. She blends grounded wisdom with spiritual insight to offer guidance that feels both practical and deeply awakening.

www.zoefox.co.uk

@zoeellenfox

We hope you enjoyed this Hay House book. If you'd like to receive our online catalog featuring additional information on Hay House books and products, or if you'd like to find out more about the Hay Foundation, please contact:

Hay House LLC, P.O. Box 5100, Carlsbad, CA 92018-5100
(760) 431-7695 or (800) 654-5126
www.hayhouse.com® • www.hayfoundation.org

Published in Australia by:
Hay House Australia Publishing Pty Ltd
18/36 Ralph St., Alexandria NSW 2015
Phone: +61 (02) 9669 4299
www.hayhouse.com.au

Published in the United Kingdom by:
Hay House UK Ltd
1st Floor, Crawford Corner,
91–93 Baker Street, London W1U 6QQ
Phone: +44 (0)20 3927 7290
www.hayhouse.co.uk

Published in India by:
Hay House Publishers (India) Pvt Ltd
Muskaan Complex, Plot No. 3,
B-2, Vasant Kunj, New Delhi 110 070
Phone: +91 11 41761620
www.hayhouse.co.in

CONNECT WITH HAY HOUSE ONLINE

hayhouse.co.uk

@hayhouseuk

@hayhouseuk

@hayhouse

@hayhouseuk.bsky.social

@HayHousePresents

Find out all about our latest books & card decks • Be the first to know about exclusive discounts • Interact with our authors in live broadcasts • Celebrate the cycle of the seasons with us • Watch free videos from your favourite authors • Connect with like-minded souls

'The gateways to wisdom and knowledge are always open.'

Louise Hay